HEAR
THEM
PRAY

FOLLOWING

THOSE

WHO CHANGED

THE WORLD

BY PRAYER

J. B. SHEPHERD

Published by J. B. Shepherd
Greenville, South Carolina, USA
SparksatTwilight.com
Printed in the USA

© 2024 J. B. Shepherd

Cover and interior design by InsideOut Creative Arts, Inc.

For additional information please visit SparksatTwilight.com or
e-mail jb@sparksattwilight.com.

DEDICATED TO THE

PRAYER WARRIORS FOR YEMEN,

WHO WEEK BY WEEK ARE WORKING TOGETHER

WITH GOD TO CHANGE THE WORLD

CONTENTS

INTRODUCTION

Buzz. *Buzz.* I glanced at my phone, and suddenly my heart rate quickened. Could it really be Marjorie?

For months I had been asking the Lord to draw her heart back to me. Ever since she'd returned to the U.S. from Pohnpei, her home island, she'd had so many uncertainties about whether to keep dating me—let alone marry me—that I had finally offered to give her all the space she needed and stop pursuing her.

It had been a hard, lonely month since then. I struggled with worry. I prayed often, but my thought patterns weren't filled with faith. Finally, the Lord gave me a breakthrough when I confessed that I wasn't trusting Him enough. I committed myself to actively meditate on His Word for three weeks, and I asked that He would do a special work in my heart so that I would be completely content in God alone.

He answered! There were a lot of ups and downs over those three weeks, but by the end I could tell that I had been changed by God's Word. I still remember with joy that twenty-first day—the last day of the three weeks. I had a song in my heart and a bounce in my step as I headed for my quiet place to read Scripture and pray. I felt that God had never been so close to me.

And *then*—not a day earlier or later—my phone buzzed. Marjorie said God had been working in her heart too, and, long story short, we've been happily married for over a decade now. *God had heard my prayer!*

Sometimes God's answers to prayer are thrilling and obvious like that. To give you another example, recently I was praying for the Lord to provide a certain dollar amount from my book sales in order to support a special ministry project. To be honest, I thought the amount was pretty unrealistic. But God worked, and when I totaled up the profits at the end of the year, the amount was almost exactly the amount I had been asking for. Wow! Moments like that become anchor points for faith ever after.

God answers prayer. He really does. That fact is the foundation of everything else in this book.

Sometimes the answers aren't as extravagant but are still special. God helps me find missing envelopes when I ask. He provides parking places right where I need them. He supplies a needed crib just at the right moment. He gives wisdom in a hard conversation. He lets the baby sleep through the night. These examples might seem trivial, but such prayers are an important part of walking with God. I'm sure you can give many more examples from your own experience.

But there are other prayers we pray—big prayers—that we pray time and again, perhaps for years, without seeing any results. Maybe you've been praying for Aunt Mary's salvation for as long as you can remember, but not a thing has changed. Perhaps you've been asking God to give you a close friend or a spouse, and yet time just passes. Maybe you pray for God to move mightily in the ministry you lead, but it feels like the people's hearts are as hard as concrete.

Twenty years ago, my three best friends and I began praying every week for God to revive our Christian school.

We longed to see an awakening like the revivals we had read about in Scotland or in America's history back in the early days. We *did* see God work in some wonderful ways in our own hearts. (A couple of those friends actually came to faith later on—I had no idea they were lost at the time!) But we didn't see the results we had anticipated.

Fast-forward to today. At the time of writing, the four of us are scattered to four separate corners of the globe—Kentucky, Peru, Cambodia, and the Middle East. Each week we gather via a group phone call to keep praying for revival, only now our burden has expanded beyond our local academy to the whole world. God has answered many of our prayers. But we're still waiting for the big awakening. Since Christ has assured us of an answer (John 14:12-14; 15:7), we're determined to keep on praying until we see it.

We know others who are praying for revival as well. Maybe you are. Or maybe you're praying for other things—huge to the world, or maybe just huge to you—and still waiting for results. These prayers are the hard prayers to pray. At least they're hard to *keep* praying with a strong faith. But I believe these are the sort of prayers above all others that this generation desperately needs. The reason I'm writing is to encourage you to persevere in and grow in such praying. If you haven't ever prayed such prayers, I'd like to urge you to begin.

Our world is in a constant state of emergency. During the time you read this short introduction, most likely someone God loves will slip away into eternal death. Some marriage will dissolve. Some son or daughter will slide into grievous sin. These tragedies take place constantly.

Ever since the fall of mankind into sin and death, our whole human race has been broken—terribly broken. People at your work and on your street live as if the true God were no more than a curse word. Some worship Hindu deities. Some worship money. Some sell their souls to Satan. Millions of people have never once heard the precious gospel. They are without hope! Has that reality become normal to you? Or can you still grieve over such lostness the way Christ did (Luke 19:41–44)?

As long as Satan's forces are at work in this world, nothing short of big, long-haul, faith-filled prayers will turn the tide. You may be familiar with the term "prayer warriors." It's a good description of what the Bible calls for. *Warriors.* God's exhortation to pray "at all times in the Spirit" with alertness and perseverance (Eph. 6:18) comes at the conclusion of the list of armor for battling "spiritual forces of evil in the heavenly places" (6:12). That kind of praying goes beyond doing our religious minimum! I believe it's the kind of praying Christ has done (Luke 22:32)— and is doing (Rom. 8:34)—and the kind He's longing to see in His people (1 John 2:6).

But such praying is difficult. It takes *faith.* That's why I'm writing this book. My goal is to strengthen your faith as well as my own in our faithful, prayer-answering God.

Maybe your prayer burden at this time is smaller than worldwide revival, focusing instead on your immediate family, your church, or your unsaved loved ones. Perhaps God has laid a special people group or nation on your heart. Maybe you're just longing for a closer walk with the Lord personally. In any case, if you're finding prayer to be hard and results to be less than expected—but you want *greater* faith (Matt. 15:28) to keep on praying even *bigger* prayers (John 15:7)—I believe this book is for you.

How will this book help? By telling stories—God's stories. God knows what we struggle with, so He answers our nagging doubts and our honest, painful questions about prayer by giving us more than simple formulas. He tells us about *real* people with pain like ours (or worse) who learned to ask and receive from Him. People like that have changed the world.

So can you. But how will stories from the past help?

The Spirit tells us through His servant Paul, "For whatever was written in former days was written for our instruction, that through endurance and through the encouragement of the Scriptures we might have hope" (Rom. 15:4). Paul had incredibly high expectations of God—enough to get up after a mob had stoned him and finish planting a church (Acts 14:19–23). Where does he say such a strong hope came from? The stories in the Scriptures. From his earliest years as a Jewish boy studying under Gamaliel, he had known God's words. He knew what the Lord had done in the past, and he had come to know that same Lord—personally—in his own day.

God's dealings with former generations were written as examples for us (1 Cor. 10:11). Perhaps as Paul sat in prison in Philippi, he thought back on God's faithfulness to Joseph, Jeremiah, or Daniel during their seasons of imprisonment. When James wanted to encourage believers in his day to persevere in prayer, he reminded them how Elijah, a man just like us, made a world of difference through prayer (James 5:16–18).

Here we are in our day, needing to pray more than ever but struggling to find the faith to cry out like our forefathers. I believe a closer look at the prayers of people such as Abraham, Zechariah, Hannah, and especially our Lord Jesus will increase your faith as you watch how God answered them. I personally find myself coming back to these stories over and over, clinging to them for fresh faith. They are the ones that God has used to change my own prayer life, and I am excited to share them.

In each chapter, we'll begin by putting ourselves in these people's shoes—or sandals—with a short narrative section that allows us to imagine the details of the scene. I want you to enter their experience as much as you can. Then we'll discuss the lesson God gives us from His Word through those stories and how it all connects to our lives. The lessons from chapter to chapter build toward a final climax in chapter 9. At the end of each chapter, I offer a tangible application that you can implement right away in your personal prayer life. Then I close with a prayer that expresses a proper response to what God has shown us.

You may be unfamiliar with finding historical fiction in a devotional book, so let me give a little explanation about the short imaginative scenes. In those sections, I purposely include details that go beyond our actual knowledge—I'm taking creative license, and I intend for you to read the material in that light. Why are those parts there? I have three reasons.

First, those short scenes provide significant insights into what we read in the Bible. Sometimes I'm simply drawing out the obvious implications. Other times I'm connecting the dots—showing how the events in that moment relate to other passages of Scripture. For instance, in chapter 2, I don't mean to imply that I know Christ's actual thoughts in Gethsemane. Rather, among other things, I intend to explain what He meant by "the cup," show the joy referred to in Hebrews 12:2, and help us connect His personal suffering with His key claim in John 14:6. Each story section focuses on a definite point; I encourage you to watch for those (chapter titles are a big clue).

Second, I think the imaginative story parts are great for helping our memory. We tend to remember experiences far better than simple information. Maybe some of you will raise an eyebrow today at my choice of hair color for a given character. Ten or twenty years from now, you may have to admit with a grin that it was the stories that really stuck with you more than anything else I said.

Finally, I'm using stories in order to reach the heart. Mere explanation mainly reaches the head. But entering into the emotional details of someone's experience—that moves us, strengthens us, and changes us. After all, God's Book isn't a mere list of do's and don'ts. He tells us people's stories. Ultimately, it's all His story. And I think explaining stories by using storytelling (doesn't that kind of make sense?) helps us avoid glossing over familiar phrasing and really engage with God's message.

This book isn't intended to be a lofty treatise. I believe it will be inspiring. It's definitely practical, as long as you're willing to try the suggestions. Even more, it's an opportunity for you to interact with the Lord Himself and get to know Him in a deeper way. May the Lord receive a host of faith-filled prayers as a result.

So let me invite you to join me. Take off your shoes now and tread lightly. We're standing on holy ground. Listen. Someone is praying. And God is there.

Father, we think of You sitting on the throne of the universe, dwelling in unapproachable light, and yet stretching out Your hands to welcome us. We praise You for our Lord Jesus at Your right hand, giving us this access. We surrender to Your Spirit, leading us to cry out to You as our Father. And we confess that we struggle when it comes to praying. Often we fall short. We still go on, but we don't always sense much closeness to You or feel much confidence in our souls that our prayers make a difference. Please come and meet with us. Please teach us to pray. Strengthen our faith. I ask that when I finish reading these stories I would be a changed person because of Your Word. I love You. In Jesus's name, amen.

1

DRAWING NEAR TO GOD HIMSELF

ABRAHAM

GENESIS 18

The hot sun warmed Abraham's neck as he watched the two angels continue on down the path into the valley. So they were headed toward Sodom. He didn't like to think what they would find there.

They went around a bend and disappeared from view. Abraham turned back toward the Lord, who still remained beside him. *What is He waiting for?* Abraham's heart beat faster. The Lord had come with the angels. But He wasn't leaving with them.

Abraham and the Lord stood at the highest point on the trail, a place that afforded a panoramic view of the lush valley spread out beneath them. Far below, Abraham could see flocks of sheep clustered around ribbons of crystal water. In the distance, the towers of Sodom gleamed in the afternoon sun. Beyond that lay Gomorrah and other cities.

As he studied Sodom's majestic buildings, a knot formed in his stomach. Scars of war zigzagged the city walls, but its beauty remained. Abraham thought back on the war when four enemy kings and their armies had taken Sodom's people captive, including his nephew Lot.

Abraham had rescued them all. The Lord, the Most High God, had enabled him to pursue and overpower the enemies with only three hundred of his servants. He could still remember the shocked faces of the people of Sodom, exuberant in their thankfulness for what he had done for them. More importantly, Lot and his family had survived. *But now?*

Abraham turned his gaze back toward the Lord. There was something overwhelming—dreadful and wonderful at the same time—that exuded from His presence. *This is God.* Abraham was certain of it, although the Lord had appeared to him in the form of a man. A heavy brown beard covered His lower face, and He wore a turban. His eyes were fixed on the city below. In a sense, He looked much like any other middle-aged tribal chieftain. But there could be no doubt regarding His identity.

He had spoken like no other man spoke. He had repeated His promise that He Himself would give Abraham and Sarah a son. He and the two angels He had brought with Him had eaten the meal Abraham served. Then as Abraham accompanied them on their way, out of the blue the Lord had made the startling announcement—He was about to destroy Sodom.

At least, He was evaluating it. But what hope could there be that He would spare such a wicked city? Abraham's chest tightened at the thought of his nephew's family perishing, not to mention all the others who would die.

But then again, why had the Lord used Abraham to spare the city before? And why did the Lord continue waiting for Abraham while the angels went on their way? He was a merciful God. He had been very generous to Abraham. And He was a just God also—He wouldn't destroy the righteous people with the wicked ones. Perhaps there was still hope after all. If there was, it could be found in only one place—the Lord Himself.

The Lord turned His eyes at that moment and met Abraham's gaze. His look was sober but inviting at the same time.

Abraham wiped his sweaty palms on the folds of his robe. His mind was made up. As fearful as he felt in God's holy presence, there was nowhere he would rather be at such a moment.

Taking a deep breath, he stepped nearer to the Lord. And he spoke to the Most High—to God Himself.

In Genesis 18:23 we read, "Abraham drew near." He got close to God. Think of that! I've been helped in my prayer times frequently by meditating on this phrase. What Abraham experienced in a physical sense is true in a spiritual sense for all those who truly pray.

Here is the point to consider—perhaps one of the most important: *the beginning of true prayer is drawing near to God.* Abraham drew near to the Lord in body and spirit. God invites us also to draw near to Him in our spirits (Heb. 10:22). At its core, prayer is a conversation with the Lord of the whole universe. It goes far beyond formal religious activity to a very personal, relational interaction with none other than God Himself.

Now just to clarify, prayer isn't *only* drawing near to God. I don't mean that as long as you have wonderful communion with the Lord, it doesn't matter whether or not you get actual answers to your requests. That isn't the Bible's message at all. The account before us includes a definite emphasis on asking and receiving (with an astonishing worldwide impact, as we will see in chapter 9). God wanted a man to intercede, and He knew that He could count on Abraham.

So prayer is more than just fellowship with God. But if we're going to change the world by praying like Abraham did, we've got to start right where Abraham started— drawing close to God Himself.

God is approachable! Although He dwells "in the high and holy place," far above the loftiest offices of world rulers, He also dwells "with him who is of a contrite and lowly spirit" (Isa. 57:15; see also 66:1–2). He appeared to Abraham in the form of a man so that Abraham could see Him face to face and speak with Him. And He makes Himself available to us through prayer.

My intent at the outset of this book is to go beyond the principles to the very heart of prayer—connecting relationally with God Himself. This chapter examines three key aspects of that relational element. First, God—as a Person—deserves our *attention* when we pray. Second, our prayers are a *response* to God communicating with us. Finally, the source of all fruitfulness in prayer is not our skill or effort, but simply *God Himself*.

Before going any further, let me draw a quick application from what we've considered already. God Himself is paying attention to you right now, eager to help you learn from this chapter. If you haven't already, stop and ask Him to teach you from what you read. I'd encourage you to begin every chapter by first acknowledging His presence and asking for Him to grow you spiritually through the reading. I am confident He will answer.

Giving God Our Attention

Abraham could have simply stood there wishing for something to change. He could have wrung his hands in worry. Instead, he turned his attention toward the Lord. Maybe he physically switched his gaze from looking out over the valley to looking straight into God's face.

When he drew near to God, he still had Sodom on his mind. But he was giving his primary attention to God.

If we're honest, don't many of our prayers fail to get off the ground right at this very point? I remember once when I tried to pray with all seventy of my English students, one by one, as they came by my office to discuss their research papers. I'm glad I did, but I have to confess that many of those times I was performing a genuine spiritual exercise without actually thinking about God at all. I was thinking about the students' research papers.

Have you ever gotten halfway (or all the way) through a prayer before you actually started listening to what you were saying? Do you sometimes realize mid-prayer that you've been speaking your wishes into the air, but the reality that Almighty God is actually listening to you with His full attention hasn't once entered your mind? Even worse, have you gone for days, weeks, months, or even years without much God-awareness when you speak with Him?

To clarify, there's no need to beat yourself up at this point for all the times you try to focus but get distracted while you pray. Keeping our minds focused is probably an area every one of us can grow in. I think we'll benefit more from finding techniques that help us make progress than from kicking ourselves. The point here is that we ought to be careful not to ignore God or take Him for granted.

There's a real danger here, especially for those of us who have attended church a long time. You know all the standard prayer phrases so well that you can rattle them off for several minutes while at the same time replaying a ballgame in your mind or having a mental argument with your spouse.

And we who are in full-time ministry must beware! Praying alone and with other people is such a part of our daily work that we can unwittingly lapse into mindless repetitions—at times even the very kind Christ warned against (Matt. 6:7). I urge all of us to examine ourselves and see how much activity we do in the Lord's ministry—even the holy act of prayer—without really engaging the Lord Himself or giving Him our full attention.

I know there have been times when I've finished a formal prayer—all the time imagining what words I would say next—and launched into preaching, counseling, or parenting without even realizing that I was doing it all in my own strength. Have you ever done that? Or worse, has such powerlessness become normal? Do you go out to serve after your prayer time like Samson went out with his new haircut, relying on experience rather than on God (Judg. 16:20)? Or instead do you glow like Moses coming down from a fresh encounter with the Lord (Exod. 34:24)? Have you learned the difference between relying on your own strength and relying on God's?

Christ told a story about two men who went to the temple to pray (Luke 18:9-14). The religious man offered up a prayer that was quite impressive—at least to some. But God was not impressed. The man was so focused on his own spiritual achievements that God

Himself never really entered into his thinking, and when he was finished he received nothing from the Lord for all his efforts.

At the same time, an unscrupulous man, whose very job involved betraying his nation, entered the temple and stood off to the side in shame. He was very aware of the presence of God—painfully aware. All the prayer he could muster was just seven words of genuine repentance, asking for God's mercy. But he got it! He had spoken genuinely with the Lord and been heard.

The Lord told that story to emphasize our need for humility in prayer. In it we find a helpful gauge to measure how well we're drawing near to Him with our full attention. If we can speak to God carelessly with canned phrases and self-confidence, we probably haven't given Him much thought. But if our hearts are moved to humility because of His holiness, we're at a good starting place to be accepted and answered.

Responding to God

As we continue to explore the relational aspect of prayer, consider another point. Before Abraham ever drew near to God in prayer, God had already drawn near to him. Abraham's prayer was a *response*—God was the one who had initiated everything.

Many years before this event, God had called Abraham into a special relationship with Himself. Abraham had responded in faith, leaving his home and people to follow God's call. God protected Abraham through many dangerous episodes, getting him out of his self-made scrapes and even blessing him with riches. In response, Abraham built altars and worshiped the Lord. We could say that Abraham's whole life was a continual series of responses: God kept initiating more grace, and Abraham kept responding by further obedience and worship.

The story under consideration is no exception. God drew near first by coming to Abraham in the form of a man to give him a face-to-face message (Gen. 18). Abraham responded by serving God and walking with Him. Then we get to listen in as the Lord speaks to Himself. He says, "Shall I hide from Abraham what I am about to do?" (18:17). Imagine that! God speaks as if He feels obligated to share His heart with Abraham.

Can you see how the Lord sets up the whole thing? It was His idea for Abraham to intercede for Sodom. He already knew in advance how He would work and how He would answer prayer. He knew He could count on Abraham to listen to Him and respond. That's why He shared what He did about Sodom. Only then did Abraham draw near to intercede.

Have you thought of your prayers this way? Prayer, at its best, is a response on our part to what God has initiated. Prayer is relational. The Lord is leading you to interact with Him about something that was on His heart before you ever thought of it.

Your whole day can be lived as a response to God. Imagine whispering, "Thank You for loving me; I love You too," to your heavenly Father as you flip back the covers in the morning. You can have a personal thanksgiving service with the Lord Jesus while you shave, cook, or drive. Whenever you're surprised by an extra window of time during the day, you can look to the Holy Spirit to see what *His* will is for seizing that opportunity.

And when you enter your prayer time, expect God to communicate with you. You're not entering a list into a machine, right? You're interacting with the Lord of heaven and earth who gave His life for you. He will direct you.

In the first place, the Spirit will use God's Word to guide you. In my experience, some of my most faith-filled prayers have happened spontaneously in the middle of my Bible reading time. The more you spend time meditating on God's Word, the more opportunity you're giving God to speak to your heart and direct you. I sometimes enter prayer with a particular verse as a guiding point—a practice I find extremely fruitful.

We think of George Müller as one of the greatest men of prayer. Do you know where such a prayer life came from? His mind was saturated with the Scriptures. By the time he was seventy-one, despite his myriad responsibilities, he had read the whole Bible more than a hundred times.

The Lord will guide you through your daily circumstances as well. As you walk with God spiritually, as

Abraham did physically, He'll alert you to key information in order for you to bring it to Him in prayer. Be watching. It's no accident that your classmate mentioned his medical need in your hearing or that a specific missionary came to speak in your church. The burden you feel for a certain outreach or particular family member may be God's Spirit drawing you to intercede, just like He drew Abraham.

When you draw near to God, you can be certain that He's the one initiating it (Ps. 27:8). He's been drawing near to you first.

The Bottom Line: God Himself

The final point about prayer's relational nature can be a huge encouragement to you: it's God Himself who makes your prayers successful. Have you noticed the way Abraham spoke with the Lord? Open to Genesis 18:22–32 and take a closer look. Here's a small sample:

> Then Abraham drew near and said, "Will you indeed sweep away the righteous with the wicked? Suppose there are fifty righteous within the city. Will you then sweep away the place and not spare it for the fifty righteous who are in it? Far be it from you to do such a thing, to put the righteous to death with the wicked, so that the righteous fare as the wicked! Far be that from you! Shall not the Judge of all the earth do what is just?" (18:23–25)

We can see tremendous wisdom in how Abraham appealed to God's character as the righteous Judge. We see great perseverance. There's also humility here, earnestness, and very specific asking without any fluff.

But do you notice as well how repetitive Abraham is? There's a depth of emotion that the Holy Spirit preserves for us in the text by not editing out all the times he says the same thing. Read those verses again out loud and see for yourself. Isn't there comfort in that observation for you?

Abraham's prayer was great not because of how literary it was, nor how focused, nor how wise. It was just that he was really talking with God Himself, and the Lord, the Most High God, was right there with him—listening and answering.

Deep down in your heart are you expecting very little to come of your prayers because you think you can't pray powerfully enough? It's true that you can't. But Abraham couldn't either. Listen carefully and take great encouragement from this. The power was not in the prayer but in the *God* he prayed to.

Think of it. We're talking about the God who designed the universe in infinite detail and created it out of nothing in a mere six days by speaking it into existence. We're talking about the God who went with a terrified Moses into Egypt and single-handedly rescued an entire nation from slavery. We're talking about the God who made water come out of rocks, split a sea into dry land, poured out fire from heaven, shut the mouths of lions, and raised dead people to life.

This is the God who became a man in order to enter death itself and break its power by rising again to save His fallen people—forever. We're talking about the Lord. What made such a powerful difference for Abraham was drawing near to *Him*!

That very same God is looking into your face right now, and He's holding out His hands to you to come to Him. You don't have to take a number, make an appointment, or get on a waiting list. If Christ is your Savior, you too, like Abraham, can draw near to Him and speak with Him.

As you begin times of prayer, I urge you to first remember specific verses, attributes of God, or stories from the Bible. Expect the Spirit to prompt your memory. Take a minute to marvel at the One you're getting ready to speak with. Ask Him to help you draw near. Let me put it this way: try to push through all the fog in your brain until your spiritual eyes meet His and you're convinced He's actively listening. It should be a humbling, but wonderful, experience.

Here is a very practical suggestion I'd like you to prayerfully consider:

> For the next twenty-one days, begin your main prayer time with at least sixty seconds of concentrating on who God is as a person. Purpose to give Him your focused attention and pray as a response to what He has first said to you through His Word.

I suggest twenty-one days because it takes about that long to form a habit. Yes, I could have said "a minute" instead of sixty seconds. But I encourage you not to cut corners, so I made it extra specific. I have found this application to be a great help to me personally, and I want to invite you to make it your practice as well, at least in principle. Even if you miss a day, pick up again and keep on going.

In my own experience, taking time to focus on God has turned boring prayer times into sweet fellowship. Instead of repeating empty wishes into the air, I've been able to genuinely ask with great anticipation of God answering.

I remember other times—far too many—of trying to pray quickly through my list and then feeling guilty afterwards that I hadn't really connected with God. So I would pray a little longer and then a little longer still, hoping the guilty feeling would go away. Usually it increased instead because I was focused on how well or how long I was performing my duty. But the times when I focused on God Himself and responded to what He said in His Word—what a difference!

The bottom line is not your skill at asking but God's graciousness in answering. If you struggle to find the right words or proper emotions but you genuinely speak with the Lord, then you can be sure of a good outcome. The Bible assures us, "Draw near to God, and he will draw near to you" (James 4:8). Won't you join me now in responding to Him?

God of Abraham, You have become my God as well, and I am glad to draw near to You. Please forgive me for all the times I've carelessly ignored You. No one is as worthy of my attention as You are! Would You please show me Yourself even more in my Bible reading so I would live with a proper awe of You? I love You and would rather have more of You than of anything else. I need Your help to grow in my relationship with You in prayer. Thank You that You will answer me. I come now and always in the name of Jesus Christ my Savior. Amen.

2

THE COST OF
MAKING A WAY

THE LORD JESUS

JOHN 14:6

I am the way."

He'd spoken those words to His men just hours before. He Himself—Jesus, the Son of God—was their way back to the Father. He had felt such joy giving that declaration. But now in the darkness of Gethsemane's garden on the outskirts of Jerusalem, the weight of becoming that way was beginning to overwhelm Him. The time He had dreaded for so long had finally come. This would cost Him everything.

Pain shot through His chest, and His breathing came only with great labor. In spite of having three men accompanying Him, He suddenly felt isolated and alone.

"My soul is extremely sorrowful," He whispered, "even to death."

Peter, James, and John looked into His face with worried expressions. They couldn't even begin to understand.

He needed to speak with His Father. He had to. "Stay here," He said to His men. "Stay awake with Me and pray so you don't enter into temptation." But He knew they would fall anyway, tonight at least.

Stumbling a little farther along the path, He found a bare place and dropped to His knees in the dirt. Balling His fists and pressing His forehead into the ground, He groaned. Anguish of anticipation that He'd held back for the last few hours—for years—came flooding out now in a heart-wrenching cry.

"Oh, Father!"

Sobs shook His frame, and He couldn't speak. He could hardly think. The time had come to drink the cup of God's wrath.

He knew that cup. That wrath had consumed Sodom, Babylon, and even Jerusalem with everything in it.[1] He had shared along with His Father those feelings of fury against people's treason, immorality, and gross violence. He could still taste the potent indignation at being betrayed by people He had created and cared for. He knew that wrath well and understood more than anyone else how much the world deserved its full outpouring.

And yet He—the innocent one—was about to drink the cup dry on their behalf.

"If it be possible," He cried, "let this cup pass from Me!"

But He had come to save His people, and there was no other way. His Father had called Him to this—to be their high priest—to give up His own blood as the sacrifice that would bring them salvation.

His stomach twisted. Large drops of sweat ran through His hair and off His face to splash in the dirt—drops red with blood. He rocked back and forth. Now scriptures were coming to mind. The Spirit was still with Him. His Father was answering His silent cries. Words of hope He had memorized as a child from the book of the law and the psalms filled Him with light. He felt a hand on His shoulder, and looking up, He recognized an angel kneeling beside Him, strengthening Him.

Now He thought of the joy He would have welcoming His people into the kingdom when He had made all things new. He could imagine their faces filled with wonder and love. He could see past them to His Father's smile of pleasure in His Son.

"I am the way."

Yes, and He would *be* that way. His blood was the only way. "Yes, Father."

His body trembled as He raised His voice toward heaven. "Not My will, but Yours be done."

He would be the way.

I chose this particular scene for two reasons. First, Christ is our ultimate example as we learn to pray, and there is much we can observe here to instruct us. In chapter 8, we'll return to this scene and unpack some key lessons. The second reason is that we need to understand how costly prayer is. That is the focus of this chapter. Giving us access to God cost Christ everything. At the risk of over-imagining, I have tried to portray in detail what the Scriptures describe so we could more deeply appreciate on an emotional level what our Savior experienced for us.

Such a holy moment between the Son and the Father may seem too painful and too private for us to venture into. Yet our Lord chose to bring His men close enough to listen, and the Spirit guided them to pass down to us what took place. God intends for us to witness this event and to meditate on it. Why? Because it happened for us, and God wants us to take it to heart.

Take a good look at the strongest of all men, groaning in anguish in the dirt of the garden. Look also at His bruised face the next day, raw and bloody with the beard torn off. Hear Him—the only man ever truly innocent—crying out as He died on the cross under God's condemnation in place of the whole guilty world. Why did He go to such lengths of suffering? Why?

Because there was no other way.

Christ's sacrifice was the only way people could draw near to God. Abraham could never have drawn near if God hadn't known in advance that Jesus would lay down His life in Abraham's place. Apart from Jesus's blood, you and I can't draw near either. Yet so often we take this great gift for granted.

The Great Dilemma

I remember asking a coworker once about his walk with God. He admitted that he never read the Bible, and he certainly wasn't very religious, but he *did* pray every day. In fact, I've met many people who told me something similar. Most people tend to assume that God listens to them just because they talk to Him (even though they never actually listen to what *He* has to say).

But in reality, a great many diligent, heartfelt prayers never reach God at all. According to Proverbs 28:9, many prayers actually disgust God; He even calls them "an abomination." There is only one way for us to draw near and have God accept us and our prayers (1 Tim. 2:5). In fact, apart from that way, coming into God's holy presence would destroy us (Heb. 12:29).

Consider our history. When God first made people and set them in the garden of Eden, He made them perfect. They got to be with God—right up close every day. Maybe some of the first prayers sounded like this: "Lord, guess what Adam found today! It was so soft and fluffy. You'll never believe what he named it" or "Thank you, God, for the different fruits. And for Eve. And just for being with us every day. I'm so happy I can hardly stand it!"

But then everything changed. Our first parents listened to Satan instead of God, and they broke God's law. Instead of running to fellowship with God as before, now they ran away from Him and hid. God came to them and clothed them, but there was no way around their sentence. Because of their rebellion, they would have to die. Their close fellowship with the Lord was broken, and they were expelled from Eden's garden and the tree of life.

"Sin came into the world through one man, and death through sin, and so death spread to all men because all sinned" (Rom. 5:12).

Skip forward a couple thousand years in history to the time of the exodus. The Lord had promised to make Abraham's descendants into a nation, and He had done it. He had multiplied them. By unimaginable miracles He had rescued them all out of slavery to the political superpower of their time. He had provided enough food and water in the wilderness for all two million of them, not to mention their vast herds of animals. And at last, He had assembled them at Sinai, the mount of God.

Future generations would look back in wonder at what took place there. God entered into a special relationship with the people of Israel. He testified that He had chosen them as His "treasured possession among all peoples" (Exod. 19:5). Then after great preparations, as the grand culmination, God put His holy presence in the very midst of their nation—He had come to be their God, *right with them.*

Yet as we read about this beautiful relationship unfolding between God and man, we can't help but notice an overwhelming tension. God's closeness—their greatest blessing—was also their greatest danger. When God manifested His glory to them on the mountain, He had to give them multiple intense warnings not to get too close. If they did, they would die.

When God showed Moses a special glimpse of His glory up close, He had to cover Moses at first so he saw only a small bit. God told him, "You cannot see my face, for man shall not see me and live" (Exod. 33:20). In fact, after severe judgment had fallen on the camp, the people of Israel concluded that anyone approaching God's tabernacle would definitely perish (Num. 17:13).

In case you think such statements are an exaggeration, come and stand a moment in somber silence before the graves of Nadab and Abihu. These two young men were some of Israel's very first priests. As sons of Aaron, they were the cream of the crop. But when they dishonored God by disregarding His instructions for public worship, His holiness consumed them in fire.

Come over now to the gravestone of Uzzah and read the epitaph. He perished in the days of King David simply for reaching out his hand and touching the ark of God's holy presence. We also find the unmarked graves of scores of Israelites who died because they looked into that ark to satisfy their curiosity. Even in the New Testament era, we find two freshly dug mounds for Ananias and Sapphira, struck down by the

Lord in front of the congregation because they lied to the Holy Spirit.

Do you feel the tension here?

The Lord loves people and wants them close. He loves you personally. He thinks about you every moment, and He longs for you to give Him your heart. But at the same time, He's so pure and good that the sins that you take lightly are as repulsive to Him as a pile of corpses smelling up your living room. That's a problem!

The Resolution

But God had a plan from the beginning—a plan to deal with sin once and for all so that He could bring us close to Him. He gave indications of it to Adam and Eve before they ever left the garden. We find more hints in the blood sacrifice of the lamb that their son Abel offered. By the time of Moses, when the Lord lived in the midst of Israel, He was making very loud—though symbolic—statements about His plans through the forms of tabernacle worship.

In order for Him to live in Israel's camp, He had to have a holy tent, set apart from the people's access on multiple levels. To approach the tent at all required a blood sacrifice, a faultless animal dying in the place of the person offering it as payment for his sins. Only the priests could go into the tent itself. Inside the tent, a massive curtain blocked even the priests from entering the most holy place where God manifested His presence.

That space could be accessed only by the high priest once a year and only with the blood of a sacrifice.

Do you see? God was picturing the way to come to Him. God's plan was to judge sin with death—not the death of the sinful people who deserved to die but the death of a pure, holy substitute—a sacrifice. The sacrificed animals were a picture of this holy individual who could die in place of all sinful humanity. By such an ultimate sacrifice, God could justly punish all sins. At the same time, He could show mercy by forgiving sinners and bringing them back to Him (Rom. 3:26). To carry out such a plan to save mankind involved the greatest tension and the greatest resolution.

Jesus was the resolution. He was the only one who could become the substitute because He was the only one in human history to live a perfect, holy life. He was the only one with the right to enter the Father's holy presence. Not only that, He Himself is in fact *God* just as much as the Father is. Of course, God wouldn't force anyone else to die for sinners. His love compelled Him to do it Himself.

Jesus was both God and man. Since He had become human, He could count as one of us and take our place. And He did.

There's no question about it. Jesus willingly went to the cross and sacrificed His life in place of yours. He took the death you deserved. God's hand of holy anger slammed down the gavel declaring Him guilty. At the same time, His hand of mercy signed your pardon. Have you personally accepted this pardon for yourself? If you haven't, your prayers have no guarantee of reaching heaven. But if you turn from your sin and trust the Lord Jesus to forgive you, the way is open. "For 'everyone who calls on the name of the Lord will be saved'" (Rom. 10:13).

The moment Jesus gave up His life, the massive curtain in the temple that separated people from God's holy presence was torn in half from top to bottom. Talk about a powerful message from God! He was welcoming us to come close to Him, even into His holy presence. He had made a *way* for us. He had given a sacrifice that could wash our sins away and make us as pure in our souls as Jesus Christ. As long as we approach God through Jesus Christ's sacrifice, we can come right into God's very presence—boldly (Heb. 4:16).

Our Response

Jesus didn't stay dead. Once He had paid for sins, God accepted that payment. Christ rose to life in a new, glorious body, and several weeks later He ascended victoriously right into heaven itself on behalf of those who trust Him.

Now we can have something better than even a high priest's access into the holy of holies in the tabernacle. God invites us to approach His actual throne in heaven (Heb. 4:16). That's where we enter—in a spiritual sense— when we truly pray through Christ. Have you come to terms with this yet? It's hard to grasp. Though in your body you may be kneeling by your bed or driving in the car, you are in fact entering the command center of the universe in your spirit when you pray. And the King is also your Father who listens to you (Matt. 6:6).

How will you respond to Christ's unimaginable sacrifice for you?

It may be that you've never truly accepted Him personally as the sacrifice for *your* sins. Maybe you believe all the truths about Him. Maybe you say prayers every day. You might have been baptized. Maybe you've been a church member for years or even a spiritual leader in a church. Perhaps you'd even say you're one of the most moral people you know.

But none of your goodness will ever get you access to God. In fact it's extremely repulsive to God when you act like you can come to Him because you're good enough. You aren't. There's only one way to God (Acts 4:11–12), and if you try any other way you'll never make it. Ever. You'll end up in eternal condemnation and outer darkness.

But when you get honest with the Lord about how sinful you are, you'll discover He's reaching out with open hands to give you forgiveness. Jesus didn't die because He had to. He wanted to. He wanted to save you, and it was worth it to Him. Are you ready to turn from your sinful life—or even your self-righteous life? Do you want a new heart? Then all you need to do is to be honest about your desperate need and accept Christ's salvation as a gift. He's waiting for you to come.

If you're ready, you can talk to the Lord right now and say something like this:

> Lord Jesus, I see now that I'm an unclean sinner and don't deserve to enter Your holy presence. If You don't save me, I will be cut off from God forever. But I believe You love me and died in my place and rose again to save me. So I'm coming right now to accept that gift. Please make me clean inside so I can please You and live for You from now on. Thank You! Amen.

Repeating these words or any similar prayer is not a spiritual formula. But if this prayer represents the very thing you want to say to God, and you haven't yet trusted Christ to save you, then you can use it. Or you can say the same thing in your own words. It's a one-time transaction (John 5:24). Jesus promised that if you come to Him in true repentance and faith, He will never cast you out (John 6:37). So you can be 100 percent sure He will answer you.

Maybe you've asked Him to save you in the past, but you aren't sure now if you truly belong to Him. Perhaps you've asked Him many times, but then you haven't loved Him and obeyed Him like you meant to. Have you ever worried that you didn't have enough faith or weren't serious enough? Maybe you worry that you're too sinful for God to ever want you near Him. Do you feel like the message of this chapter just confirms those worries?

Let me offer you some encouragement from someone who knew Jesus Christ better than most. The apostle John lived with Jesus for several years before the ascension and continued to follow Him for the rest of his life. As an old man, he testified, "If anyone does sin, we have an advocate with the Father, Jesus Christ the righteous. He is the propitiation for our sins, and not for ours only but also for the sins of the whole world" (1 John 2:1-2). God put it in the Bible as absolute truth.

There are a couple of key words in this verse that deserve an explanation. "Propitiation" tells us that Jesus's blood totally succeeded in meeting God's holy requirements to punish sin. All sin. "The sins of the whole world." Period. And this same Jesus is your "advocate." That means that if you've put your case in His hands, He's on your side. You belong to Him. He sits right next to God the Father all the time on your behalf (Rom. 8:33-34), so if there ever arose any question at the throne about whether or not you belong there, Jesus would cover for you: "This one is mine."

You may not remember the date of the day you first trusted the Lord Jesus. But it doesn't matter. Do you want to love and follow God? Then don't worry about nailing down a point in the past. You can love and serve God right now as long as you're trusting in Jesus. If you know you've disobeyed in some way, then you need to confess it and ask for fresh cleansing. The Bible promises us as God's children, "If we confess our sins, he is faithful and just to forgive us our sins and to cleanse us from all unrighteousness" (1 John 1:9). So come with bold hope to the throne through Jesus Christ, and don't be afraid.

Maybe in your case, you've been saved for many years, and you know it without a doubt. You might be able to explain the gospel better than I have. Does this message about Christ being the way have any significance for you?

It does if you're human.

As a young person, a parent, or even a pastor, don't you sometimes struggle with taking prayer for granted? I know I do. Since we pray multiple times a day, and since we don't have to dress up, stand up, or even speak up in order to reach God in our spirits, we sometimes treat this holy opportunity as something trivial. We can begin to go through the motions without showing the Lord much respect at all.

Even worse is the danger of neglecting prayer altogether and the precious access to God for which Christ laid down His life. He opened the way for us to come right to God Himself and live our whole lives in close contact with Him. It cost Jesus everything. He is eager and willing to answer our prayers, but we are tempted to forget and rush from one activity to the next by our own efforts, never taking time to give God our full attention. Often, He gets no more from us than a lot of "quick prayers" or none at all. But isn't Christ worthy of our time?

I'm sure that Satan's forces are very intent on hindering our prayers. Why do we face so many distractions when we try to focus on God? Why does it seem so laborious to speak with our loving Father? Why is it so hard to gather

God's people for a prayer meeting? I think the ultimate reason God's dear children shrink back from such a glorious opportunity is that it is a matter of intense spiritual warfare.

But the fact that Jesus is the way gives us a decided advantage over our enemy because that's a sword of truth that can cut temptation short. The enemy will tempt you to skip (or rush through) prayer. But you can remember Jesus's agony in intercession the night before His death in order to give you that privilege now. Think about it! How can Satan's lies succeed against such a reality? If your coming to the throne was so precious to Christ that He would go to the cross in order to get you there, then prayer isn't something you want to pass up. It isn't something to hurry. And the prayer meeting is the grandest privilege in the week.

Do you ever feel like God is annoyed at your coming? Do you think He gets tired of you? Never! He would rather die than have you stay away—and that's exactly what He did do in order to make the way open. He loves you. He welcomes you. He has paid the ultimate price to make the way.

The Lord Jesus is the way—for you.

Dear Father of our Lord Jesus Christ,
how utterly humbling it is for me to
meditate on Your holiness. It's even more

humbling to think of Your Son's suf-
ferings for me and how much You've
loved me after I've hurt You so deeply.
Please forgive me for taking prayer for
granted, treating You disrespectfully,
and often even neglecting to seek You
altogether. The enemy fights against
me so hard when it comes to praying,
and to be honest, I really struggle. I'm
sorry for all the times I've backed down
instead of standing up to the attack
and honoring Your sacrifice. The love
You showed me compels me afresh to
make praying a top priority. I purpose
to draw near to You and stay near from
now on, but I need Your help. Please
keep the price that was paid for this
way before my mind and embed it in
my heart. I love You. I come to You in
Jesus's name—and only in His name.
Amen.

3

BLESS ME TOO!

JABEZ

1 CHRONICLES 4:9–10

I say it's time we act!" Jabez gestured toward the fertile valley. He could smell the trees in blossom and hear the gentle bubbling of a nearby brook. He stood with his uncle and cousins on a slope in their tribal inheritance, looking out on the Jebusites' territory—their feet planted in the dirt atop a slight ridge. Jabez searched his relatives' faces for any sign of agreement.

"You mean you want us to actually fight to get that piece of land?" Malchijah said, his thick, black brows furrowed above a deep frown.

"Of course!" Jabez fought to control his exasperation. "The Jebusites are our enemies, and they're occupying our land that the Lord gave us."

Zabad snorted. "Help yourself, cousin. But I think I'd rather watch from a distance." He adjusted his belt around his bulging middle.

"What do you expect us to do?" Malchijah's eyes flashed with anger. "You want us to grab our pitchforks and go running off after you right into enemy territory just to get sliced up and left for the birds to feast on? How'd you like to explain that one to my wife and kids?"

Uncle Eliashib laughed and rested his hairy hands on the shoulders of his two sons as he looked Jabez in the eye. "Your father warned me you'd try to rope us into some kind of plan like this. Jabez, you've got a good heart, but you're young and inexperienced. The kind of operation you're talking about could get complicated and deadly. No one is going to take you seriously, and there's no way you're going to fight an armed force like the Jebusites all by yourself. Be content with what the Lord has given you already."

Jabez could feel the fire burning in him again, just like each time he'd spoken with his brothers—the fire of frustration. The old fire of pain. "That is the land the Lord has given me—that He's given to all of us in Judah."

"Look," said Zabad. "If you just want land, old Elah's got more than he even knows about. Just budge the landmarks a little, and you can get yourself whatever you want without going off and making trouble for everyone."

"No! That's against the law. And you're missing the whole point." Jabez gripped his short sword even tighter in his left hand as he raised his fist with the right. "The Lord tells us that if we just obey Him, He'll go with us. Remember Caleb? I say we—"

"Forget it." Malchijah cut him off. "You'll only get yourself more pain, Jabez. Your mother birthed you in pain. Your name means pain. You'd think by this point you'd try to avoid it rather than seeking out more of it."

"And being a pain to the rest of us," Zabad added with a grin.

The three men laughed and headed home, leaving Jabez alone on the ridge. His heart sank as he watched them disappear. For a while he paced along the border, head hung low, kicking rocks out of his path. Why did it always go like this?

Finally, he plopped down on a fallen log. The aroma of blossoms mixed with the smell of distant wood fires. Enemy fires. He traced lines in the dirt with the tip of his sword and began quoting to himself once more the words he'd memorized as a young child—the story of how Father Jacob wrestled with God, never letting go until he got the blessing. That's when his name was changed to Israel—the one who strove with God and prevailed.

How I wish He would change my name too!

Lifting his head at last, he stared into the sky above the enemy territory before him. Groaning, he spoke aloud: "Oh God of my father Israel, oh God—my God, won't You bless me as well? Please help me expand my borders so I can possess the land You've given us. Please let Your hand be with me, like You promised Father Israel that You would be with him. You blessed him so much, and yet in my case everyone thinks I'll come to harm and have nothing but pain. But I'm clinging to what You've told us. Won't You please protect me and give me success so that all their dire predictions will come to nothing? Please answer me. I'm calling upon Your name and putting my trust in You."

He wiped his blurry eyes and drew in a long breath. Now what? Only God knew what He would do in response. But one thing was for sure—Jabez had asked. God would do something.

The Bible says of Jabez,[1] "God granted what he asked" (1 Chron. 4:10). No details are given—no story of brave deeds or battles won. The Spirit—the Master Author—opts to cut out the whole climax in order to state the moral of the story as emphatically as possible. In short, Jabez prayed for God's blessing, and God said yes.

Isn't there something profound in the very simplicity of that? Buried in the lists of genealogies that surround it, this one man's name and story stand out above all the others in his day. Why? Because there's a message here we need. God loves this story, and He's eager to do something equally amazing in your life. Here's the message: if you want God's blessing—particularly in your service for Him—ask Him for it!

The Lord teaches us, "Ask, and it will be given to you" (Matt. 7:7). He says again, "If you ask me anything in my name, I will do it" (John 14:14). Several times that final night before Christ's crucifixion, He stressed to the disciples the need to ask in His name. At last He said once more, "Ask and you will receive, that your joy may be full" (John 16:24). From Christ's perspective, asking God is no insignificant matter.

Now maybe if you read Jabez's prayer at a quick glance, you might think Jabez was rather selfish. I've actually heard his story preached as an example of what *not* to do. After all, he's eager for more real estate and protection for the sake of his own comfort, right? But the clues in the text lead me to take quite the opposite view. Go ahead and read the actual words from the Bible.

> Jabez was more honorable than his brothers; and his mother called his name Jabez, saying, "Because I bore him in pain." Jabez called upon the God of Israel, saying, "Oh that you would bless me and enlarge my border, and that your hand might be with me, and that you would keep me from harm so that it might not bring me pain!" And God granted what he asked. (1 Chron. 4:9–10)

First, notice that God opens by declaring from His own vantage point that Jabez was "more honorable than his brothers." Second, God concludes by saying that He did what Jabez asked. Also, when you look at those requests closely, you can see there's a lot more going on than someone merely seeking a comfortable life.

Our Generous Father

Let's start with Jabez's general request: "Oh that you would bless me!" Was Jabez selfish to want God's blessing? It depends on your view of God. Do you think of Him as a crotchety, impoverished neighbor who would rather not be bothered by your requests for help?

Or is God like Caleb, a generous father loaded with hard-won blessings for his children? When Caleb's daughter asked him for a field as a bridal gift, he gave it to her gladly. He'd conquered the land, and he had plenty to give. Although his son-in-law may have been reluctant to ask for such expensive real estate, Caleb's daughter knew her daddy's heart. When she requested a further blessing of "springs of water," he went above and beyond, giving her both "the upper springs and the lower springs" (Josh. 15:18-19).

The fact is, God is very much a loving Father like Caleb, and He delights to give good things to His children. When the Son came into the world to reveal God so we could know Him, God's fatherly heart was one of the greatest points Christ emphasized. He speaks of God as "Father" more than a hundred times in John's Gospel alone.

When the Lord Jesus taught His disciples how to pray in the Sermon on the Mount, He began, "Our Father." Why? He gives us further insight later in the sermon:

> Which one of you, if his son asks him for bread, will give him a stone? Or if he asks for a fish, will give him a serpent? If you then, who are evil, know how

to give good gifts to your children, how much more will your Father who is in heaven give good things to those who ask him! (Matt. 7:9–11)

Christ wants us to see God as a good Father who gives to us when we ask. When Jabez asked God to "bless" him, he was right on target. *Blessing* pretty much sums up what God especially enjoys doing for His children.

The moment God created people in the beginning, He blessed them (Gen. 1:28). When He entered into a special relationship with Abraham, He blessed him, and ultimately He blessed the whole world through him (12:1–3). When Jacob wrestled and prevailed with God, what did he win? God's blessing (32:29). God's blessing is the very thing Christ gave His life to procure for His people, so that the Father has "blessed us with all spiritual blessings in heavenly places in Christ" (Eph. 1:3).

In fact, one of the greatest honors you can show God is to ask Him for His blessing. For instance, before spending hours trying to master your speech for school or the next business meeting, spend time humbly asking the Lord for His guidance and enablement. Before buying yet another self-help book to figure out how to babysit your energetic grandchildren, spend some significant time on your knees. Make prayer the priority (and not the afterthought) at your church committee's business meeting.

Too often God's children turn every other direction for blessing first, when all the time their Father is holding out His hands for them to come to *Him*. It's actually pride and distraction on our part—not selflessness—that keep us from asking for God's blessing.

So God gives us Jabez as a role model. You can cry out just like he did, "Oh that You would bless me!"

A Prayer for Expansion

But what about this specific request for more land: "Enlarge my border"? Doesn't that sound a little self-ish? It might seem so on the surface. There are certainly people in our day who offer up self-serving prayers. Scripture says they ask but don't receive because they just want to satisfy their selfish cravings (James 4:3).

But Jabez's prayer is different. When we understand what God had commanded the people of Israel, his request makes sense. It also gives us direction for our own asking and receiving.

At least forty-three times in Deuteronomy, God spoke to Israel about possessing the land. He promised it to them, just as He had promised it to their father Abraham over four hundred years before. He swore to give them the land (Deut. 19:8). He emphatically urged them to go up and take it (1:8). In fact, three times He specifically testified that He would extend their borders—the very wording Jabez used in his prayer (Deut. 12:20; 19:8; Exod. 34:24). At that time, expansion was one of Israel's highest callings—perhaps we could call it their primary mission. The book of Joshua unfolds the success of the people when by faith they went up and took the land.

Sadly, though, we read in the book of Judges that the tribe of Judah reached a point when they stopped driving out the Canaanites and possessing the land they had been allotted. They had done great in the mountains, but at last they concluded that their enemies in the valleys were just too much for them "because they had chariots of iron" (Judg. 1:19). At that turning point, the whole nation headed downhill. The other tribes quit trying to oust the Canaanites. They concluded they couldn't do it. But God had a different perspective on the situation: "You have not obeyed my voice. What is this you have done?" (2:2).

So Jabez wasn't a land-hungry empire builder. Rather, he was a man of faith. He saw that God had called the people to much higher things than his contemporaries were willing to get involved in. When he prayed, "Enlarge my border," he was asking for success in the mission God had given his people. He wasn't complacent. He chose not to settle for the status quo when God had promised so much more. No wonder God says he was "more honorable than his brothers"!

And God said yes to Jabez. He stretched out His hand to Jabez and expanded his borders. He kept him from disaster. And He made sure this prayer was recorded in the Bible so we could learn from Jabez's example.

The Mission in Our Day

Now how do we apply Jabez's example in our generation? God hasn't promised to give us more real estate. But He is just as passionate in our day about expansion—expanding His kingdom. Have you considered how much expansion actually means to Him? Christ gave His life to build the kingdom—a kingdom of His own redeemed people. And He didn't stop at death and resurrection. Even now He's working nonstop to rescue people all over the world from Satan's power by making them His own. He's preparing a perfected people to populate His perfect city. His mission involves tremendous spiritual warfare and sacrifice, but in the end He'll succeed gloriously!

Amazingly, He's carrying out this mission through us as His representatives on earth. He told His followers after His resurrection, "As the Father has sent me, even so I am sending you" (John 20:21). What does that sending look like? He told us to go and call people from among every people group to believe in Him and follow Him, baptizing them and training them to obey His Word (Matt. 28:18-20). The Lord has been making that mission succeed. His kingdom is spreading all across the world!

But just as the people of Judah in their day reached a point when they drew a line and said, "We can't," have we also stopped short? On a worldwide scale, millions of people live and die without ever hearing the gospel even one time. For example, consider Yemen, an Arab nation on the south side of Saudi Arabia. Out of the approximately 30 million people who live there, over 99 percent of them are Muslim. The government makes it illegal for Yemenis to convert to Christianity and for outsiders to try to convert them.

The case is similar in Oman, Somalia, Libya, Tunisia, Iraq, Algeria, Morocco, Mauritania, and so many other Muslim countries. Then there are Hindu nations and Buddhist nations and outright pagan nations. The territory God has given us to possess for His kingdom lies abandoned in so many cases because of modern "chariots of iron" (Judg. 1:19)—seeming impossibilities. But if we take the Lord's command seriously to make disciples in "all nations" (Matt. 28:19), we must own our responsibility to spread the gospel to those difficult places and reach them soon before another generation perishes.

And what about your community? Your neighborhood? How many of your classmates or coworkers will spend eternity in the lake of fire? It's an overwhelming thought, so if you're like me, you might feel like wriggling out from under the burden and finding a way to reason yourself back into a state of settledness. Many believers conclude that as long as they're trying to reach some folks here and there, they're doing enough. If they participate in outreach and give to missions, that's even better. But when it comes to hoping and praying for *many* souls to be saved through them—or even one specific person—many hesitate. Maybe you do.

Yet in Jabez, God shows us an encouraging example. What if we had a burning heart like Jabez did? What if we embraced the Lord's zealous love so much that we couldn't be content to let our neighbors perish? What if it pained us to have no more than a handful of people saved in our church over the course of a year? And then, what if we asked God?

What if we definitely, expectantly, specifically, and persistently asked God to enlarge our borders?

I'm sure you do at times. But isn't it hard to keep asking with great faith? Often, it doesn't appear that our asking brings any different results. Lost people stay lost. Outreach gets boring. People we love—perhaps even our own children—remain hardened. So it becomes tempting to stop asking with great expectations.

We come up with reasons to explain why our "borders" are so narrow and will likely stay that way. "This generation is just too hardened." "God just wants us to be faithful." After a bit, we begin to actually feel virtuous for praying vaguely and not being overambitious or presumptuous. We might even get the idea that as long as we're having good fellowship with God when we pray, it doesn't matter so much whether or not He says yes to our requests.

But the Lord Jesus envisioned the whole thing far differently.

It was the night before He died. His men were scared because He was about to leave them and put the weight of His mission on their shoulders. But He told them not to be afraid and gave them an astounding plan for victory. Just listen to His words:

> Truly, truly, I say to you, whoever believes in me will also do the works that I do; and greater works than these will he do, because I am going to the Father. Whatever you ask in my name, this I will do, that the Father may be glorified in the Son. If you ask me anything in my name, I will do it. (John 14:12–14)

Doesn't that sound like He intends to say yes when His disciples ask for things? He says, "I will do it." Not only that, it sounds like asking and receiving are at the heart of His strategy. He says that when we believe in Him, we'll do His works and even "greater works." How? We ask for whatever needs to be done, and He'll do it. Do you see? This matter of asking and receiving is crucial to the whole advance of Christ's kingdom.

One of my favorite missionary stories is the account of James Fraser, who labored tirelessly for years at great personal sacrifice among the Lisu people of southwestern China, preaching and teaching from village to village. He saw very little fruit initially. Yet he grew in faith and in prayer through the process. A key part of his story is that, back in England, his mother gathered a team of prayer warriors who labored earnestly in prayer for him. Out alone on those Chinese mountains, he was laboring in prayer as well.

The Lord gave Fraser the faith to ask—in a very definite way—for thousands of Lisu to be saved. He believed that God had answered yes. Still, there was no response among the Lisu for quite some time. He was just about to give up and find a new location. But as he took one final tour, the Spirit of God poured out the long-awaited salvation, and people were actually running to him from villages before he even got there, begging to hear the message so they could be saved. God did indeed save thousands over the following years and multiplied churches of Lisu believers all over that remote region.[2]

Don't give up. Perhaps you see the hardness of hearts and feel the heaviness of trying so often to reach souls, to train your children, or to accomplish any other ministry God has given you. You may feel like there's no hope except to settle back and lower your expectations like the children of Judah, who stuck to the mountains and left the valleys alone. But here through the story of Jabez, God invites you to ask Him to bless *you* as He has blessed many others before.

I've focused especially on soul winning in this chapter as an essential part of Christ's mission to build His church (Matt. 16:18). Building up one another as believers is also a crucial part of that mission (1 Cor. 14:12). In all the forms of ministry God calls you to, He invites you to pray for expanded borders—for even greater spiritual fruitfulness than ever before. It may not come all at once or in the way you anticipate. (We'll talk about some of the painful complexities in the following chapters.) But the foundational principle God wants us to start with is that when we ask for success in His calling, He plans to say yes.

For the main application point of this chapter, I'd like to offer you a resolution to make. Can you prayerfully purpose this with me?

> I resolve not to settle for less in my service to the Lord where He is promising me more. Instead of whispering "Never mind" in the face of impossibilities, I will open my mouth wider.

The focus here, as in Jabez's prayer, is on the mission and promises of God. You may have caught the reference to Psalm 81:10, where God exhorts His people to open their mouths wide for His blessing. If you can make this resolution with me, you might find it helpful to post it on your office cabinet, fridge, or backpack.

Do you suppose Jabez ever imagined that his story would be impacting your life several thousand years later? I doubt it. God enlarged not only his physical territory but also his influence—far beyond anything he ever could have guessed!

That's the way God is. He rewards those who diligently seek Him, and not just a little bit (Heb. 11:6). Which verse will become the summary of your ministry? Will God say, "You do not have, because you do not ask" (James 4:2)? Or will you receive "far more abundantly than all that [you] ask or think" (Eph. 3:20)?

The Lord Jesus calls you now: "Ask, and you will receive, that your joy may be full" (John 16:24). What are you waiting for?

Dear God of Jabez, the God of Israel—and my God, I come in love to You as my Father. I marvel at how You've blessed people of faith in past generations, and I cry out, "Please bless me too!" I confess that too often I fail to ask, but by Your grace I want to be more faithful. Please strengthen my faith and the faith of Your people around me. Your Son deserves to have a multitude of new followers from our generation, and so for His sake, please help us reach many more souls. Please let Your hand be with me and enlarge my borders. In Jesus's name, amen.

VICTORY THROUGH INTERCESSION

MOSES

EXODUS 17:8–16

Moses gave a start as Aaron touched his elbow.

"Are you even listening to me, Moses?" Even though the two brothers were now both in their eighties, Aaron's voice still had that sharp edge of an older sibling.

Moses stopped climbing and leaned on his long staff, his sides heaving. "I'm sorry, Aaron. It's—it's just hard to focus right now."

He looked back down the dusty brown hill to where their friend Hur was following them. Beyond him at the base of the hill, thousands of goatskin tents spread out as far as his eyes could see—tents filled with people. The Lord's people.

"They're counting on me, Aaron."

"What?"

"All of them. It's been only days since we crossed the Red Sea, and now death is staring us in the face again. They're counting on me to rescue them. But what can I do?"

Distant shouts filled the air. War shouts. The Amalekites had found them yesterday and attacked the back of the line, where they were weak. How many had died already? The Amalekite warriors were trained killers. The people of Israel were just farmers and bricklayers—not to mention mothers, children, and many elderly. Faces came to mind. *It isn't fair for them to attack our weakest members.* The people were exhausted; this couldn't be happening!

Old doubts about God's calling pulled his heart down into his sandals. *The Lord promised.* They'd seen Him work miracles! But at every turn there came another problem, and now some of the people were getting butchered.

"There." Aaron pointed at the line of Hebrew soldiers running behind Joshua, the young man Moses had sent to fight the Amalekites. "They're so few."

"Our hope isn't in numbers." Moses tightened his grip on the staff. "Come on. Let's go up higher where the soldiers can see us better."

"What good will that do? Are you going to signal to them?"

"Not exactly. But they need to see." Moses took off once more. Aaron hustled after him, gasping for breath. "Wait! I don't understand."

Moses stopped and gazed out across the dusty plains once more. "I'm going to lift up the staff of God."

Aaron came up beside him and stared into his eyes but said nothing.

"If God doesn't intervene, then it's all over, right here!" Moses hadn't meant to shout. *But it was true! If God didn't act now . . .*

Moses turned his head so Aaron couldn't see his face. "The Lord promised that He'd redeem this nation, and He said to take this staff to use for doing His miracles. Remember the plagues? Remember how I stretched out this staff at the Red Sea? This is the staff God told me to use for giving us water out of the rock. Miracles! We need another miracle from God."

"But how? What did God tell you to do?"

Moses let out a deep breath. The Lord hadn't given him any specific instructions in this case. *Why?* There were things about this attack that didn't make any sense. He felt intimidated by Aaron's questions. But there was one thing he *did* know—he needed God. So did Joshua.

"Moses?"

"I'm just going to hold up this staff."

"Is that what the Lord told you?"

"No. I mean, not really. But I've got to reach Him! Don't you see? I'm going to hold this staff over my head until He does something. We can't do this without Him."

I've got to reach the Lord.

"But you can't keep it up all day, Moses. Your arms will give out."

Moses took a deep breath and started hiking again. He barely felt the inner strength to even lift the staff, let alone keep it in the air. But the people were counting on him. Joshua and his men needed him. He sure hoped he wasn't wrong about this. The people needed to see that it was *the Lord* who gave the victory.

"I'll hold it all year if I have to."

Lord, I can't do this. Please answer me. You're the only one who can help us.

By the end of the day, Joshua and his men had totally overcome the Amalekites. Moses's arms ached, and Aaron and Hur were no doubt exhausted as well from standing on each side to support his hands. But don't you think Moses's heart felt lighter? God had answered him and delivered the people once again.

Here's the exact account.

Then Amalek came and fought with Israel at Rephidim. So Moses said to Joshua, "Choose for us men, and go out and fight with Amalek. Tomorrow I will stand on the top of the hill with the staff of God in my hand." So Joshua did as Moses told him, and fought with Amalek, while Moses, Aaron, and Hur went up to the top of the hill. Whenever Moses held up his hand, Israel prevailed, and whenever he lowered his hand,

Victory Through Intercession

Amalek prevailed. But Moses' hands grew weary, so they took a stone and put it under him, and he sat on it, while Aaron and Hur held up his hands, one on one side, and the other on the other side. So his hands were steady until the going down of the sun. And Joshua overwhelmed Amalek and his people with the sword.

Then the LORD said to Moses, "Write this as a memorial in a book and recite it in the ears of Joshua, that I will utterly blot out the memory of Amalek from under heaven." And Moses built an altar and called the name of it, The LORD Is My Banner, saying, "A hand upon the throne of the LORD! The LORD will have war with Amalek from generation to generation." (Exod. 17:8–16)

What did Moses do? In one sense, he simply held a special piece of wood over his head. But more than that, he connected with God on behalf of people who desperately needed God.

This wouldn't be the last time he obtained grace for others. Not long after the account we're considering, Moses fasted for forty days while he pleaded with God to show mercy to the people of Israel. God used Moses's intercession on that occasion to spare the nation from destruction over the golden calf incident (Deut. 10:10–11). In Jeremiah's time, nearly nine hundred years later, the Lord still remembered Moses as one of the greatest intercessors in Israel's history (Jer. 15:1).

Wouldn't you like for God to use you as well to obtain His grace for His people? We saw in the last chapter that God delights to bless you when you ask. But how much do you believe that He'll bless *others* when you ask?

Can you think of anyone who needs God's help right now? What about your husband or wife? You probably know better than anyone else your spouse's depths of pain and human weakness. Don't you long to see God's grace abound in his or her life? Will you play a part in obtaining that grace? Maybe you have a child your heart aches over. The fact is, every person you know needs God's constant grace—great grace, and as soon as possible.

But here comes the big question: *can you really change their lives just by asking God?*

The apostle Paul was confident that it could be done. He earnestly wrote to new believers in Thessalonica, Colossae, and Ephesus to pray for him and his companions. He told the Corinthians that their prayers would play a critical part in God's work of deliverance for him (2 Cor. 1:11). And be encouraged—he wasn't writing to a spiritually mature audience.

James was convinced as well. He wrote that the prayer of a righteous person accomplishes *a lot* when it's set in motion. No wonder he told the believers, "Pray for one another" (James 5:16).

John urges us to pray for sinning brothers with the expectation that God will answer us (1 John 5:16). Peter knew by experience the power of intercession because Jesus had prayed for Peter when he had failed (Luke 22:32), and God graciously restored him to a fruitful walk and ministry.

So the witness of Scripture is clear. Praying for people works. But how does it work? Can it really work for you? And to what extent?

Can you, for instance, actually impact a missionary's safety because of a specific prayer? Can you make a difference in your pastor's relationship with God and in the power of his Sunday messages just by asking God? Will people you've never met—even people from another country—approach you in heaven someday and say something like this: "The Lord told me that I came to faith because of your prayers. Thank you!"? Can your prayers help your friend's marriage? What about a homeless person in need of work? Or perhaps hardest of all—that wayward family member you've already been praying about for twenty years?

This account God has given us of Moses lifting the staff offers us so much help in answering such questions. For one thing, God gives us a very tangible illustration. We can get our brains around what's happening here because God uses physical objects and an agonizingly real crisis. Second, we find two fundamental principles in this story that apply not only to his situation but also to our questions about the matter of intercession. Taken together, these two principles provide a powerful picture of getting God's grace for those in need.

Principles of Intercession

First of all, just before we dig in, notice the context. The setting is a battleground. This story doesn't happen in a laboratory, much less in a flower garden or lecture hall. War is ugly. It's gut-wrenching for the people involved. I'm thinking right now of families that go into panic at dinnertime if a plane flies over their house. I'm thinking of a teenage boy dragging dead bodies off the battlefield and suddenly realizing that the soldier he's dragging is his own uncle. It hurts to think about war when it's for real.

Only God knows the agony Moses went through as he stood on top of that hill and lifted the staff. It's good for us to keep that point in mind because our context for interceding is war as well. Perhaps you haven't had to experience the horrors of physical war, but I'm certain you've experienced the horrors of spiritual war.

This world is not at peace. People all around you and in your family carry deep wounds. I have friends from high school who used to worship the Lord with me and have since repudiated Christ to pursue the world. I can think of several friends whose marriages have crumbled. I've spoken with hundreds of hopeless taxi drivers who have never heard God's message of salvation. People need help!

So the Lord gives us these two principles of intercession that worked in Moses's hour of need. They will also work in our time of need.

Principle #1: Faith Is the Victory

Faith is a significant word that we need to discuss before we see it in the story. It goes along with *grace*, another significant word that can be difficult to picture.

As I study these terms in the Bible, the best picture to help me understand them is that grace from God is like His great hand reaching down to offer us something. He gives us life, love, protection, the ability to do good, and so much more—that's grace. We don't deserve it. But He is a God of grace who loves to give, and He even calls His throne "the throne of grace" (Heb. 4:16). We come to that throne when we pray to get the help we need.

Faith is like our little hand reaching up to receive what God is giving us. That's about all there is to it. It's the way we receive forgiveness, eternal life, and every spiritual blessing we need. It simply takes God at His word and receives the grace He's reaching out to offer.

Now do you see why I say "faith is the victory" in this story? Joshua and his men were fighting their hearts out on the battlefield, and yet from the divine record it's obvious that their skill level didn't really make any significant difference. Everything depended on Moses's staff. If the staff went down, the Amalekites started winning. When the staff went up, the tide turned.

How did a piece of wood make such a difference? It didn't. That lifted staff simply represented that Moses was reaching out to God. That staff was called "the staff of God" (Exod. 4:20; 17:9). The Lord had told Moses to take it into Egypt in order to use it to "do the signs" (4:17). Whenever Moses used it, people would know that it was *the Lord* at work, and not Moses.

So when Moses held up his hands, the extended staff was an expression of faith. Moses was depending on the Lord, and God responded with a glorious victory. Moses's outstretched faith received God's outstretched grace.

What would expressing faith look like in your life? I imagine you aren't running outside to find a big stick. Perhaps at times you run to obey the Lord's commands, just like Joshua ran to the fight. Certainly his obedience was a critical expression of faith.

But I believe the primary expression of faith for us is *prayer.*

As Christ's disciples stood gaping at the fig tree He'd just withered, He told them,

> Have faith in God. Truly, I say to you, whoever says to this mountain, "Be taken up and thrown into the sea," and does not doubt in his heart, but believes that what he says will come to pass, it will be done for him. Therefore I tell you, whatever you ask in prayer, believe that you have received it, and it will be yours. (Mark 11:22–24)

Faith precedes amazing works of God—even miraculous ones. But did you catch the action point? Christ said those works happen when you "ask in prayer." He also said on another occasion that whoever believes in Him will be the channel for Christ's even greater works. How? "If you ask me anything in my name, I will do it" (John 14:12-14). A little later He told them, "If you abide in me, and my words abide in you, ask whatever you wish, and it will be done for you" (15:7).

In the book of Hebrews, we're welcomed to come through Christ to the very throne of grace—God's throne in heaven—to get mercy and grace at the moment we need them (Heb. 4:15-16). Chew on that awhile. Do you want to go out and change the world? We need to. We're commanded to. The Bible is emphatic that we must go to all people in every place to proclaim the gospel. But the most important place you can ever go—before anywhere else— is to the throne of God Himself.

Moses in his time of need reached out his hand to God's throne, and he received all the grace necessary for an overwhelming victory. The grace wasn't just for Moses—he got grace for the men in the battle as well, and even for the entire nation! How did that happen? It worked because of the second key principle related to intercession.

Principle #2: God's Work Is Teamwork

It's so beautifully obvious in this story. The victory of faith came by everyone working together. They had to depend on each other.

The nation of Israel *needed* Joshua's men to go out and fight for them. But without the lifted staff, Joshua and his men would have been butchered. They *needed* Moses to intercede for them. Yet Moses couldn't keep his hands up. He *needed* Aaron and Hur to hold up his hands. None of the men in this story could have succeeded alone, but because each one did his part, they all came home to their tents singing that night.

Maybe at times you feel like Elijah did when he was depressed and complained that he was the only one left who really loved the Lord. But the fact is, you're not alone. It's a good thing because, in a very real sense, your spiritual vigor is dependent on other believers around you. Other believers are dependent on you as well.

The New Testament speaks of believers in Christ forming a spiritual body. Paul uses a humorous illustration to make the point when he says that the eye can't say to the ear, "I have no need of you" (1 Cor. 12:21). All the parts of the body are interdependent, and so are the members of Christ's spiritual body. It's humbling but extremely helpful to realize that our spiritual strength is determined in part by the prayers of others.

Even the apostle Paul knew he needed brothers and sisters to pray for his boldness (Eph. 6:19) and for his success in ministry (2 Thess. 3:1). How convinced are you of your need for others' prayers?

Picture yourself in Joshua's shoes in the thick of the battle. Sweat is dripping into your eyes. Every muscle is strained and stinging. A wound on one arm is bleeding, and you're trying desperately to block sword strokes that you can hardly keep track of. Now up on the hill you spy Moses in your peripheral vision. He's letting the staff sag. Suddenly you're thrown on your back and about to die. But the staff goes up and just as suddenly you're filled with new energy.

I think that if you went through that experience, you'd come away convinced that intercession works—fully persuaded that God responds.

Maybe that mental picture can help you be more earnest and honest in asking others to pray for you in your spiritual battles. And maybe it will help you feel how great the need is for you to pray for your loved ones who are also in the thick of the fight "against the spiritual forces of evil in the heavenly places" (Eph. 6:12).

Are Your Hands Lifted?

Someone down in the battle is counting on you to hold up the staff. His or her victory may depend in part on your intercession. Would you be willing to thoughtfully consider now which people God has placed in your life for you to pray for? I'd like to offer some suggestions.

First, if you're a parent, your children need your intercession. Even though you might faithfully teach them and pour your life into them, without God's grace they'll never win their spiritual battles. I remember an evangelist testifying that his mother's prayers were the tool God used to break his rebel heart when he was a teenager.

Then again, parents need intercession as well. Maybe you feel overburdened by your father's rules or your mother's interference. Have you prayed for God to give them wisdom in decision-making or confident trust in His care for you? The closeness of family life provides the best vantage point (and greatest responsibility) for praying for each other.

What about praying for your pastor? Like Moses he feels the tremendous weight of responsibility for the souls under his care, including yours (Heb. 13:17). His ministry—including his prayer life—has a tremendous impact on you and your whole church. Do you ever pray for his spiritual strength? His preaching? Do you have a specific time set aside each week to intercede for his spiritual victory? What about praying for your other spiritual leaders? You want them interceding for you, and they need you to intercede for them.

Maybe you've already thought about praying for missionaries. Have you considered using their prayer letters to help you pray? The more details you learn, the more your heart and mind will be engaged in your praying. Also, you'll be able to apply specific promises of Scripture to their situations. The Spirit can guide you to specific requests that match their definite needs. Then when you read of them winning battles that you prayed about, your faith will be strengthened.

Here's another thought. How do you view the church prayer meeting? Is it just for elderly saints or those who can't serve in any other way? Is it a spiritual exercise reserved only for super-saints or extroverts (but not for you)? Based on what we've learned, the prayer meeting is as vital to your church's success at its mission as Moses's staff-holding was vital to Joshua's battle success. If at all possible, you need to be there. Pastor Bill McLeod told his Canadian congregation that they might perhaps have to miss a Sunday meeting on occasion, but the only excuse for missing the prayer meeting was death. No wonder the great Canadian Revival of 1971 began from that church.

Many other examples could be given of people needing prayer in your circle of influence and even far beyond in places not many ever think of. Why not ask the Lord to guide you in knowing which ones He wants you to give particular attention to?

I'd like to conclude with a practical application that may really help you.

> This week (preferably today), choose some specific blocks of time for intercession and write them into your regular schedule.

Maybe at the moment you feel on fire to go pray for others. But watch out! Life has a way of piling up so many responsibilities that in a few weeks you'll look back and find you never actually succeeded—unless you schedule your praying and then follow through. Perhaps your daily routine is unpredictable. In that case, you could connect your intercession time with another activity; for example, you could pray every day before lunch. One way or another, you've got to block off that time for God and for those who are depending on your prayers.

In Exodus 17, after the dust of battle had settled and the victory was secure, God told Moses to write this account as a memorial for Joshua and others in the future. The war with Amalek wasn't over. It would last for hundreds of years throughout Israel's history. The people would need to always remember these key principles—God's plan for winning their battles.

Listen. The sounds of war are all around us in our day. God has told us that faith—faith in Him—is what brings the victory, not only for ourselves but also for others. People are counting on you. Hold up the staff!

Lord Jesus, You are the master Intercessor. Through Moses's example, I see a glimpse of what You are like—saving me to the uttermost because You ever live to make intercession for me. I praise You that my ultimate spiritual victory is assured by Your hands that never falter on my behalf. Thank You! You have called me in Your Word to join You in this ministry of intercession, and so

I offer myself again today to pray for others. Please show me when to schedule my prayer time and which people to pray for. Please deepen my conviction that intercession works. Our generation desperately needs You. Please give me faith and determination to take hold of all the grace You're eager to pour out on us. Thank You. My eyes are on You, Lord. Amen.

HOPING AGAINST HOPE

ZECHARIAH AND ELIZABETH

LUKE 1:5–25

So this is it.

All his life Zechariah had imagined this moment, wondering if he would ever be chosen for such a special service. And now here he was, alone with the Lord inside the very sanctuary of His holy temple on Mount Zion.

He gaped at the room's towering golden walls and at the vast curtain disappearing into the shadows far above him. His footsteps echoed as he approached the golden altar of incense. His old fingers trembled as he lifted his censer.

Oh Lord, hear our prayers. Turn Your people to You and restore our fortunes.

Would the Lord receive his offering? The handful of incense represented the prayers of the nation. Zechariah thought of the crowd gathered outside for worship in the temple courts behind him, waiting until he came out. He thought of his dear wife, Elizabeth, back home in the Judean hill country. No doubt she was praying too. God always heard her prayers—except maybe the big one.

He reached out and sprinkled the special incense into the small flame. Immediately, a large plume of smoke arose, surrounding him with the most pungent and beautiful smell he had ever known.

He stepped back and watched the curls of smoke wafting up into the darkness. Darkness. Nagging doubts tugged at his heart. An old wound. Why hadn't God given them a child? Did He really answer prayer?

He pushed the doubts away as he had many times before. *I do believe the Lord! I will lift up my prayers for our nation with hope.*

He started to turn and leave when suddenly a man dressed in shining white appeared beside the altar, staring at him. Zechariah's heart leaped into his throat. *An angel!* His knees quivered, and he nearly dropped the censer.

The angel held out a reassuring hand. "Don't be afraid, Zechariah. Your prayer has been heard."

He took a deep breath and let it out slowly. God must be assuring him through a messenger that He'd accepted the incense. But why? *This isn't typical, is it?*

The angel went on. "Your wife Elizabeth will bear you a son, and you shall call his name John."

Zechariah's body jolted. Wait! The angel meant *his* prayer? Zechariah and Elizabeth's prayer? Surely not *the* prayer! He'd given up on getting an answer to that request years ago.

This time his trembling fingers couldn't stop the censer from clattering to the floor.

Do you feel the tension of faith and doubt here? Of course, this little narrative relies highly on sanctified imagination. But in the scriptural record, both trust and doubt come through in bright colors. Zechariah definitely struggled. He questioned how he could know the angel was really telling him the truth. As a consequence of his unbelief, he didn't get a chance to speak again until after baby John was born many months later.

But notice that God heard his prayer and gave him an enormous blessing. Surely God had seen faith in this couple. And when the child came, notice how Zechariah's faith was demonstrated. He named his son exactly what God had told him. Then the Holy Spirit filled Zechariah, and the godly old priest poured out words of confidence in God's plan for the nation and in the fulfillment of all His prophecies regarding the Messiah.

Just as Gabriel predicted, the outcome of this story was tremendous "joy and gladness." Faith—enduring faith despite significant doubts—was rewarded. Zechariah and Elizabeth's personal prayer for a child played into the turning point of all history as their son came as the forerunner of God's Son, the Savior of the world.

"Your prayer has been heard" (Luke 1:13), the angel said.

I believe we need the encouragement of this story. I come back to it often and find fresh grace from God in it. Don't you need encouragement too?

The fact is that despite all we've seen in the previous chapters that ought to make prayer the most exciting thing we ever do, it often isn't. Perhaps the hardest part is that most of the time we don't see any immediate results. We might cry out with earnestness, but we don't see hearts changed the next day. It's easy to feel like a small boy fishing with his father for hours without actually catching a fish.

Even harder is the reality that we often get confused and even feel hurt at times by how God answers our prayers—or appears not to for a very long time. Just recently after I preached about Moses lifting the staff, a sweet elderly lady approached me. She confided that even though she loves speaking with God, she finds it quite a struggle to intercede for others. Many years ago, she poured out her prayer to God for someone, and since she didn't see the answer she expected, it hurts her now to ask for anything else.

Can you relate to her experience? Do you still carry wounds that come from disappointed prayers? When I spoke about God saying yes in chapter 3, did the message touch a painful nerve in your heart?

Perhaps if no wounds come to mind you've already learned the joy of resting in God's wisdom, authority, and goodness. But could it be instead that you haven't risked praying for anything specific enough and big enough to allow for the possibility of disappointment? Have you held back from praying with the boldness of Jabez because you're afraid God's answer might actually lead to *more* pain instead of less? I think God puts up with a great deal of vague prayers that come up to Him from His children.

From the message He sent to Zechariah, though, we gather that there had been nothing vague about the priest's request. It had been definite and persistent. No doubt, over time, Zechariah's feelings about it had become quite painful. Or calloused.

Decades of Waiting

In my imagination, I picture Elizabeth and Zechariah's prayer taking place in three scenes, all around a simple, rough-hewn wooden table. In the first scene, I see a young couple giddy with newlywed excitement. They're leaning across the table toward each other, holding hands and praying, smiling at the prospect of God giving them children to raise for Him. They're full of anticipation and great expectations.

The second scene takes place ten years later. Zechariah's black beard is huge by now, and Elizabeth's bright eyes are heavy. There are premature creases on their foreheads. Elizabeth sits and toys with her long hair while Zechariah paces, a fire in his eyes.

"Our nation is so blind!" he says. "Justice hides in a corner while oppression runs rampant. When will the day of redemption come? When will we see the prophecies fulfilled?"

Elizabeth nods. "The food's getting cold."

Zechariah drags his chair out, sits facing her, and takes her hands. "Let's keep on crying out for God to turn the hearts of His people. Let's pray for Him to send us a prophet as He did in the old days—one like Elijah. Won't you join me?"

"Yes, but—"

"What?"

"What about *our* prayer too?"

Zechariah nods. "Of course. I haven't forgotten. Let's pray for God to give *us* a son who will impact this nation and turn the hearts of people to repent."

"Do you really think He'll give us a son?"

"I'm sure of it. I can't explain why, but I feel like God has given me faith about this very thing. We've waited for many years, but God will give us a son. I know He will. Let's pray for him to be a man who impacts our people."

In the third scene, Elizabeth's hair is streaked with white. She sits at the table alone with her forehead resting on her arms. Zechariah shuffles into the room, his beard shorter and grayer. Elizabeth looks up for a moment, tear lines running down her flushed cheeks. When Zechariah sees her face, he rushes to her.

"What is it, darling?"

She sobs for a while. At last she says, "I guess I always thought there was still hope. Maybe God was just waiting like He did with Abraham and Sarah."

Zechariah looks around the room, searching for some clue to her meaning. She must be saying something about their old prayer for a child.

Elizabeth groans and rests her head against her husband. "I've reached that time, Zechariah. We won't be having a baby."

Zechariah sinks into a chair next to her. "I guess I hadn't thought about it for a while. So strange how the Lord works. I was certain He was going to give us a son." He sighs. "Perhaps I misunderstood how He was answering."

Now years later, Gabriel speaks to him in the temple and says that his prayer has been heard. What a shock! What staggering news. What good news!

The Bible doesn't tell us all the details of what this couple went through. We don't know whether or not Elizabeth had reached that physical point of no return. But we do know that God did something amazing and totally unexpected. He'd been listening all that time, and He intended to answer—in far bigger ways than they ever could have guessed (Luke 7:28; John 1:6–7, 23).

What does this story teach us? Many lessons, for sure. But a big one stands out to me: *don't give up on God hearing and answering.*

The Last Minute (or Beyond)

You've probably faced many experiences that tempted you to quit. Have you had dashed dreams? Prayers that appeared to be rejected? If you start praying big prayers like the heroes of faith did, you will face those experiences at some point. But the Father is sharing the story of this dear couple's pain so we can know the outcome of their faith—and ours. *He hears us.*

Just think of all the backstory to this statement that Elizabeth made (probably to Mary): "Thus the Lord has done for me in the days when he looked on me, to take away my reproach" (Luke 1:25). Most of her adult life, she'd had to live under "reproach." Perhaps her mother and sisters were disappointed in her. Perhaps neighbors asked provocative questions or even assumed the couple didn't want children. Maybe she and Zechariah felt the unspoken accusations of friends—if they were really as godly as they seemed, why didn't God bless them with children?

They may have struggled with guilt at times. Why wasn't God pleased with them? Why didn't He answer their prayer?

And yet the Bible's record is clear. God was pleased with them. He wrote it for the whole world to read: "And they were both righteous before God, walking blamelessly in all the commandments and statutes of the Lord" (Luke 1:6). Blameless before God! Some people are righteous before others, but God says that even from His divine perspective, this couple was a model of godly character.

Are you feeling reproach and discouragement right now? Are you wondering why God has given you such a burden for something and then seems to have ignored your prayers? Have you moved on and become calloused?

It's always possible that some sin has hindered the answer from coming (Ps. 66:18-19). Ask God to reveal any such hindrance. Be honest here. Even though Job was one of the godliest people on earth, God still did a work of sanctification in his life through the trial he faced.

But if you've prayerfully listened to the Lord, and He hasn't shown you anything wrong, expect to receive a good answer! Persevere with renewed passion. Don't listen to the lie that claims He's angry but won't tell you the reason. He's a loving Father, and if He chastens you, He'll make sure you know why. If He's not pointing out a problem, He may just be waiting to answer your prayers in ways you'd never even guess.

Many of the great accounts of answered prayers are stories that involve intense waiting. Remember the outpouring of salvation among the Lisu in China I mentioned in chapter 3? That huge answer came only as James Fraser was preparing to move to a new field. Remember the story I told in the introduction about God restoring to me the heart of my future wife? That happened only after a year of intense pain as I waited on the Lord (and barely held on at times). I imagine that even Jabez had to endure a lot of waiting before he fully experienced the fulfillment of all he'd asked for.

In fact, God seems to find special delight in pouring out His blessings at the last second (or even when it looks like it's too late). Joseph had to wait for over a decade in both slavery and then prison before suddenly being ushered into a place of supreme power. Moses had to reach the very brink of the Red Sea before the Lord opened a way. Abraham was a hundred years old before God gave him Isaac. Lazarus was already dead for four days before Jesus arrived to raise him. Do you see a pattern?

Right now my wife and I are still waiting for God's answer to a trial about which we've prayed for over eight years at this point. We're not completely sure what God has in mind or what He will do. He has definitely been sanctifying us in the process. What we do know is that He has heard us and will do what is *best*.

Maybe you also have been waiting for years for God to answer an important prayer. Don't let your faith grow dim before you discover that answer. God may be using this waiting time to grow your faith for even bigger blessings—not because He's upset, but because He delights in you. I'd like to suggest another prayer habit that I believe can really encourage you.

> After each daily prayer time, pause and think of God as your Father responding to you, "Your prayer has been heard."

This is a new habit I've been cultivating in my own prayer time. Too often in the past, after praying awhile, I would fade from praying into focusing on my work instead of reaching a good close. Sometimes I would come to the end of my prayer time feeling unsatisfied that I'd really accomplished anything. But ever since I began slowing down to give God my full attention and to listen to Him telling me, "Your prayer has been heard" each time, my faith has been encouraged.

If you don't feel confident that He's heard you—even though you've come clean about any sins—then meditate on His assurances in the Bible. One year I tracked how many times the psalms mention that God hears and answers prayer. See for yourself. I'm sure I missed some, but you get the idea.

Psalm 4:3	Psalm 65:2
Psalm 6:8	Psalm 66:19
Psalm 10:17	Psalm 69:13, 33
Psalm 17:1, 6	Psalm 77:1
Psalm 18:6	Psalm 81:10
Psalm 20:1, 5, 6, 9	Psalm 86:7
Psalm 21:2	Psalm 99:6, 8
Psalm 22:24	Psalm 102:1, 2, 19, 20
Psalm 28:2, 6	Psalm 116:1, 2
Psalm 31:22	Psalm 118:5, 21
Psalm 38:15	Psalm 119:26
Psalm 40:1	Psalm 120:1
Psalm 50:15	Psalm 138:3
Psalm 55:1, 17, 19	

It is true that sometimes God says no. In chapter 9, we'll explore the nature of unanswered prayers—or ones that appear unanswered to us. There's even more encouragement to be found in God's Word. But for now, let's take this assurance that came to Zechariah when he least expected it: "Your prayer has been heard."

Keep trusting God.

"O you who hear prayer, to you shall all flesh come" (Ps. 65:2). Yes! I come even now in spite of my doubts because You have assured me that You listen and answer. I praise You for hearing little people like me. Thank You! I ask for one thing now that I greatly need. Please strengthen my faith day by day through Your Word. I want to have a diamond-hard confidence that You hear me, care about me, and plan to act. It's such a marvel that You're actually listening to me even at this moment. I love You! I come to You with thankfulness and expectation. In Jesus's name, amen.

If you can really pray that from your own heart, listen. "Your prayer has been heard."

GOD CARES ABOUT
OUR EMOTIONS

HANNAH

1 SAMUEL 1–3

Hannah stumbled down the well-worn path back to the tabernacle, the blistering sun beating down on her head. She was drenched with sweat beneath the folds of her long garments. Most people in Shiloh were no doubt napping after the midday meal, but a few still passed by. She turned her face away from them, hoping they wouldn't see her tears.

Her stomach churned and made a loud rumble. She hadn't eaten since early yesterday. How could she? This yearly trip to Shiloh always brought with it fresh waves of agony.

Why does Peninnah have to be so cruel? And why did Elkanah have to marry that woman anyway? Wasn't one wife good enough for him? What's wrong with me—the one he already had?

She stopped on the path as a sob wracked her body. Of course there was something wrong with her. She could still hear Peninnah's harsh voice: "The Lord has closed your womb, Hannah. He's closed your womb."

And her husband could be so clueless about her pain! He'd asked her, "Am I not better to you than ten sons?" When she left, he'd been bouncing one of Peninnah's little boys on his knee and smiling. *How can he smile?*

But perhaps Elkanah was right. After all these years it was obvious that the Lord had chosen not to give her children. Couldn't she just accept that fact and move on? Maybe it was time she resigned herself to childlessness and quit letting herself hurt so much.

She could see the tabernacle entrance now. The old priest Eli sat by the doorpost, his hands folded across his large belly and his eyes half open. He nodded with a smile to a man leaving the courts. If only she could smile again. Maybe she shouldn't come in bawling and making promises as she'd imagined. She could just say a quick prayer of thanks instead and head back to the family. If she just accepted her lot, perhaps one day she could feel at peace with it.

No!

She couldn't. Surely God would see her affliction and do something. Surely He would respond to her tears. He just had to.

Staggering forward in grief, she stood before the doorposts of the tabernacle, as close as she could get to the place God had chosen for His dwelling. She closed her eyes and tried to imagine the Lord listening. Was it acceptable to be so emotional in His holy place? Did God really care? Did He notice her need when He had so many bigger issues to handle?

For a while tears fell freely, but no prayer came. Then at last the words all overflowed in a torrent. She poured out the agony of her soul, trying to find some way to express how terrible the hurt was without actually dishonoring God. She suddenly realized that she'd been gesturing with her hand and even mouthing the words while praying silently from her heart. She clutched her hands together, but she couldn't stop herself from rocking back and forth.

"O Lord of hosts, if you would just see my affliction and remember me and not forget your servant . . ." She paused, thinking once more of the Nazarite vow in the law. Should she go on? Yes, she had to. "If You will give your servant a son, then I will give him to the Lord all the days of his life, and a razor shall never come on his head."

She kept on praying, speaking from her heart to the Lord about her hopes for the future. Sometime between beginning and ending, the peace she had long sought finally came. She didn't know how. But it came. She had cast her burden on the Lord. By the end of the day, when she returned to Elkanah, she was actually smiling and ready to eat once more.

Eli—though judging her wrongly at first—had assured her of God's answer. At least he had offered his wish that

God would answer. But she was sure of it. The Lord had heard her. As she closed her eyes in sleep that night, she felt as if God Himself were smiling upon her.

Yes. The Lord did care.

Are you, like Hannah was, bearing a great weight of grief or disappointment? Sometimes my heart has ached so much that I couldn't even pray except to say, "O Lord, please help," over and over again. At times like that—especially after years of praying with still no answer—it can be very hard to feel that God cares. How should you respond?

In the account we're considering, 1 Samuel 1–3, God contrasts two people who both had carried long-term griefs. Hannah was yearning for a child. Eli was longing for his wicked sons to fear the Lord. Hannah responded by intensifying her prayer. Eli, on the other hand, grew calloused. In the end, one of them got an answer from God. The other did not.

As we study their contrasting examples, we learn that God welcomes us to bare our hearts to Him. He not only allows such fervent praying, He encourages it. If we withdraw from Him emotionally, we risk the danger of becoming spiritually calloused and missing out on what God might otherwise give us.

Calloused Prayers

The bits and pieces we have of Eli's story convey a picture of a man who had grown calloused. At times, pain leaks out in this father's pleas to his boys, now young men:

> Now Eli was very old, and he kept hearing all that his sons were doing. . . . And he said to them, "Why do you do such things? For I hear of your evil dealings from all these people. No, my sons; it is no good report that I hear the people of the LORD spreading abroad. If someone sins against a man, God will mediate for him, but if someone sins against the LORD, who can intercede for him?" (1 Sam. 2:22–25)

But the other scenes give hints that he had hardened his heart to the pain. For one thing, the narrative emphasizes Eli's major misunderstanding. He thought Hannah was drunk! Why couldn't he recognize true grief when he saw it expressed? Perhaps the sight was as rare in those times as it is in our churches today. But Eli should have not only understood Hannah—he should've been right there next to her, crying out to God himself!

Then notice what Eli asks his sons in the appeal above. "If someone sins against the LORD, who can intercede for him?" (2:25). The answer he obviously expected was, "Nobody." But if he had followed Moses's example—or Christ's—he would have shouted in response to that question, "I will intercede! I will pray for you!"[1]

God gave Eli at least two prophetic warnings of impending judgment because of his sons' wickedness and his own failure to discipline them. One came through a veteran prophet (2:27-36) and the other through the young boy Samuel (3:11-14, 18). If Eli didn't catch God's intent the first time, then he ought to have understood the second time. God was giving him a chance to repent and have the sentence reversed!

When the Lord promised Nineveh that He would destroy it in forty days, the king fasted and dressed in sackcloth and commanded the whole city to follow his example. God changed the sentence (Jon. 3:10). When the Lord told Moses to step aside because He was going to destroy Israel for their idolatry, Moses prayed instead. He begged God to remember His reputation. God changed the sentence (Exod. 32:9-14).

But when Samuel told Eli that God was going to do such a terrible work that every ear that heard about it would tingle, what was Eli's response? "It is the LORD. Let him do what seems good to him" (1 Sam. 3:18). Not long after, his sons were killed in battle, the ark of God was captured by enemies, and Eli himself died in response to the evil tidings. Do you think that was really what God wanted in His heart?

It seems that Eli is a Class A exhibit of being *calloused*.

Calluses—generally speaking—are a blessing from God. I remember one summer in Oman when I got a new pair of sandals. For a few days my toes were on fire, but once the skin hardened up, I didn't feel the pain anymore. Calluses came to the rescue.

Calluses can help our hearts as well when we learn to endure heavy burdens without becoming discouraged. But when we allow calluses to make us stop praying with heartfelt emotion, we make a grave mistake. Eli appears to have lost hope. Though perhaps he still said routine prayers, he failed to persevere in expectant faith, instead resigning himself to a miserable future.

Hannah didn't let her heart grow calloused. Take a minute to read 1 Samuel 1. You can see there was nothing shallow about her words. Rather, she *intensified* her prayers. She wept. She refused to eat. She went to the tabernacle again. She made a vow. She poured out her heart with tears. She brought her deep wound to God and laid it bare before Him.

God responded to Hannah by giving her a son who eventually led the whole nation back to the Lord and anointed the first two kings of Israel. What an honor!

No doubt all of us would like to see ourselves in Hannah's place. But if we're honest, our tendency toward calloused-ness is probably stronger than we'd like to think. I know I've experienced that process. Years ago, someone I cared about turned away from God. I remember the initial pain and the earnest prayers—even fasting. But over time, the intensity subsided. The pain hurt too much to keep opening the wound. Nothing appeared to be changing. So the prayers turned into an emotionless ritual. Recently, the Lord has been convicting me of my need to revive the intensity I once had in praying for that loved one. Are there some prayers like that in your life as well?

A God Who Feels

Perhaps one reason we tend to become calloused—one you might not have considered—is that we fail to fully appreciate God's emotions. That's right—God's emotions. We can't see God's face in a physical sense. We can't hear His audible voice. It's challenging for us to pick up on the emotional signals we normally rely on to read how someone feels. So we may be tempted to assume that He doesn't feel strongly about our situation.

Add to that challenge the fact that God is perfectly self-controlled. We know that He isn't surprised. He doesn't experience shock or fly off the handle. He doesn't get discouraged. He controls all His circumstances. He is the perfect model of a righteous judge who evaluates based on the facts and not on His feelings. So when we imagine Him listening to our prayers, we might be tempted to picture Him as an impersonal bank teller—or even worse, an ATM—who simply calculates a wise response based on some divine algorithm that can't be altered.

You may find yourself asking at times as Asaph did, "Has God forgotten to be gracious? Has he in anger shut up his compassion?" (Ps. 77:9).

But God isn't like an ATM at all or even a stoic bank teller. He's like the very best father you could imagine, full of intense compassion for His children. He is moved by our emotions, and He responds with deep emotions of His own. (Where do you think our emotional capacity came from?) We can't see the tears in His eyes or hear the grief in His voice, but there is a way we can still know how much He cares: He has communicated His emotions in the Bible.

Listen to Him speak about His wayward child: "Is Ephraim my dear son? Is he my darling child? For as often as I speak against him, I do remember him still. Therefore my heart yearns for him; I will surely have mercy on him, declares the LORD" (Jer. 31:20). In Hebrew, the word translated "heart" is actually "bowels." Our Father describes His emotional pain as if His stomach were twisted. That's a lot!

Can you hear the heaviness of pain in His voice when He responds to Moses, "Oh that they had such a heart as this always, to fear me and to keep all my commandments, that it might go well with them and with their descendants forever!" (Deut. 5:29)?

God's passion and intense feelings run all through the Scriptures. The Old Testament is especially rich with stories and expressions in God's very voice that reveal His heart of compassion. Isaiah writes of God's Spirit being grieved (Isa. 63:10). David says that God shows compassion on His people like a father would (Ps. 103:13) and collects their tears in His bottle (Ps. 56:8).

Then we get an even closer look at God's heart in the New Testament, revealed in human flesh in the person of His Son. In Christ we see God reaching out a pure hand of healing and love to touch a disgustingly unclean leper (Matt. 8:2–3). We see Him telling an adulterous woman in a place of utter humiliation that He forgives her (John 8:2–11). We see Him actually marveling with joy in response to a centurion's sincere faith (Matt. 8:5–10).

And then let the weight of these two precious words from John's eyewitness account sink in: "Jesus wept" (John 11:35). He wept! He knew that Lazarus would rise from the grave. He knew the story would end well. He knew that He had done the right thing in letting Lazarus die, just like wise parents make choices their children don't understand because they love them. So why did He weep? Because Mary and the others around her were weeping, and He was moved to the point of grief in His own spirit.

Do you ever doubt God's emotions? Perhaps right now, like Martha and Mary, or like Hannah, you're in a season of suffering and completely baffled. Why isn't God responding to you? He *is*. He is planning something better than you expect (Rom. 8:28; Jer. 29:11), and He is also responding in His heart to your emotions. You may not be able to see that response, but it's still there all the same. God's emotions are deep and strong, and He has a vast heart of compassion for His children's pain.

"He cares for you" (1 Pet. 5:7).

Intensity in Prayer

Through Hannah's story, God encourages us to open our hearts to Him. We don't need to hide behind a put-on smile—God wants us to be honest. He isn't an implacable judge demanding perfect decorum—although He deserves our respect. Rather, He's "the Father of mercies and God of all comfort" (2 Cor. 1:3). When we are tempted to grow calloused and merely go through the motions of prayer, God welcomes us to intensify our praying instead.

The Bible gives us many examples besides Hannah's of such intensity. When Nehemiah heard about Jerusalem's desolate condition, he sat down and mourned for days with fasting and praying (Neh. 1:4). Ezra responded to the sin of the people by tearing his clothes, pulling out some of his hair, weeping, fasting, confessing, praying, and throwing himself down in front of the temple (Ezra 9:3–5; 10:1). When the baby that David had fathered with Bathsheba was on the verge of death, David lay all night on the ground and fasted, apparently for seven days (2 Sam. 12:15–18). Hezekiah turned his face to the wall and wept bitterly as he prayed when he heard that he was about to die (Isa. 38:2–3).

Our Savior, the Lord Jesus, is our greatest example. He prayed with great joy at times (Luke 10:21). But at other times He prayed with tears (Heb. 5:7). Sometimes He labored in prayer all night (Luke 6:12). Before His final sacrifice, He prayed in such grief that His sweat came out like blood. Even now we can be sure that He pleads for us in heaven with His whole heart, just as the Holy Spirit prays "with groanings too deep for words" (Rom. 8:26).

God has given different people different personalities, so intensity may not look the same for you as it does for someone else. David writes that he flooded his bed with tears every night (Ps. 6:6). But Heman the Ezrahite describes his experience of grief without once mentioning crying. Rather, he testifies that he continued in prayer "day and night," "every day," and specifically "in the morning" (Ps. 88:1, 9, 13). Maybe he cried as well, but from what is recorded, intensity in his case looked like sticking it out instead of giving up. Keeping a tender heart in prayer may look yet a different way for you.

Often, you may feel completely emotionless, especially the more tired you are. Sometimes in the past, I have been discouraged by what seemed like heartlessness on my part. Now, at such times, I am learning to accept the fact that feelings come and go. I try to relax and just honestly let the Lord know that I don't feel much inside—but also that I really do mean business about what I am asking. *His* feelings are the factor that makes the difference, not mine.

However intense prayer fits with your personality or with your mood, the need is still the same. Yield your heart to God's Spirit, and pray with whatever sense of fervency He gives you. He will keep you from becoming calloused.

Stirring Up the Coals

Our emotions, more than other parts of our prayer life, can be easily impacted by factors outside our control. In this regard, we have to trust God's sovereignty when we don't feel the same as others or when our feelings don't *feel* the way we think they should. However, there are a few things that we are responsible for, and when we yield to the Lord in those ways, we tend to get our emotions more in line with God's. I'd like to offer three suggestions that may help you maintain a proper fervency.

First, try to give yourself enough time. There are no shortcuts to intense praying. Hannah didn't shoot off a one-minute prayer on the fly while she was folding laundry. She hiked back to the tabernacle and stood there for a length of time to thoroughly lay out her case before God.

Do you invest the time in prayer that it takes to get emotionally involved? Do you ever stay long enough to feel the relief of leaving that burden before God? Just to clarify, I don't think most of us have the capacity to labor on the same level for every need. Some situations call for brief prayers. But I am confident that God entrusts all of us with *some* needs that He wants us to *labor* over as Epaphras did in his prayers for the Colossians (Col. 4:12).

Second, be committed. Notice that Hannah made a vow and followed through. She wasn't just reading God her wish list without any level of commitment on her part. She actually released to God's service the very son she was asking for! If you're asking God to save your coworkers, are you also asking Him to help you do a Bible study with them—and taking steps to do it? What's your commitment level?

Finally, for some prayer requests, the Lord may burden you to include fasting. Hannah fasted. Getting an answer from God was more important to her than eating. Not so for Eli. He benefited from the succulent meat stolen by his sons from God's offerings (1 Sam. 2:29). He protested against their sin, but it was hard to let go of his comfort. Oh, what he lost because of it!

Are you willing to give up eating for a time in order to really cry out to God about a matter? Christ expected His people to fast (Mark 2:20), and He assured us that our Father would see our fasting and reward us openly (Matt. 6:16–18). That's a promise.

So here's the hands-on challenge for this chapter:

> **Plan a specific time next week to fast and pray about a specific matter Christ lays on your heart.**

Maybe you've meant for a long time to get serious about praying for your Sunday school class or about a possible job change. Here's your opportunity to start. If no particular burden comes to mind, I'd urge you to make *that* your first serious matter of prayer and fasting. Ask God to reveal any areas in your life where you've been developing an Eli heart. Seeing those calluses may be the first step toward obtaining great future answers to prayer.

Maybe you're not sure how to fast. The Bible doesn't provide a handy how-to manual with detailed instructions. Rather, God gives us a great deal of flexibility because it isn't the food that's so important. The humility and purpose in the heart are what really matter. But as a practical help, I'll share a few examples of what I've seen that might give you some ideas.

Some people skip eating for an entire day or even for many days in order to pray for God's direction about big decisions. (They might even fast from drinking anything as well, up to a point.) Some fast at times for just one meal in order to hide away and pray for a friend in trouble. I know a couple that gave up putting sugar in their coffee for a month as they prayed about the struggles of one of their children. That may not even register as fasting for some of you, but for them it was a serious reminder to pray!

A friend pointed out to me that if you fast for several days, it may be exactly what is needed, but you may not *feel* much emotion or intensity—in fact you may feel far more dead emotionally than usual because of physical weakness. That's okay. What matters is your sincerity before the Lord. Persistence at such times is a definite testimony that God has given you a true fervor in your spirit.

My wife and I once did a study of every direct reference to fasting in the Bible. I've included in an appendix some further thoughts based on that study. I believe if you study the references yourself, you will be strengthened in this spiritual discipline and find great benefit from it.

In conclusion, I want to leave you with two encouragements. First, don't be afraid to draw near to God with your deepest emotions and bare your heart to Him. You will never find anyone more patient to listen, more understanding, or more deeply moved with compassion. Your Father cares for you.

Second, intense praying like Hannah's is eternally worthwhile. I acknowledge that it is not a leisure sport. It isn't fun. My flesh doesn't like fasting one bit. Taking time to pray from the heart may even open you at times to greater pain. So why go to all that trouble?

The answer is that the pain will be rewarded when you see God's grace poured out in people's lives. "Those who sow in tears shall reap with shouts of joy!" (Ps. 126:5). Christ suffered in prayer and even in death for you because of the "joy that was set before him" (Heb. 12:2). Having you in His family was worth it to Him! Are there no friends, neighbors, family members, or even nations worth your tears today so you can rejoice with them throughout all eternity?

Fasting isn't forever. Tears won't last in heaven. Praying with intensity and pain is an offering you can give to God only on this side of eternity. Will you give Him that offering?

Dear "Father of mercies," I worship You with awe because of Your compassion. No god of the heathen nor any

*mere human ever loved like You love.
Lord Jesus, thank You for entering
into our brokenness as a fellow human being and knowing our pain by
intimate experience. Thank You for
caring with all Your heart. I believe
Your assurance—"Blessed are those
who mourn"—because the grievous
battle against evil will soon give way to
eternal victory. But I confess that my
heart shrinks back from mourning, and
I shield myself and my pet comforts by
tolerating calluses. Today I ask that You
would reveal those calluses and gently
help me to open my heart to others' pain
in my prayers so that someday their joy
and mine with Yours will be far greater.
Thank You that You will surely do it. In
Jesus's name, amen.*

PRAYING BIG

DAVID

PSALM 72:1-20

As soon as the foreign envoys were gone, King David dismissed his servants and made a beeline for the sunroom in one of the eastern towers. *I need to be alone with the Lord.*

The cold air in the dark stairwells cut right through his robes to the core of his being. But the words of the envoys cut even more sharply. "Little kingdom indeed!" David grunted to himself. "They think the glory of God's nation is nothing but a temporary dream that will pass away with my dying? Bah! Old age hasn't finished—" He overstepped and nearly tumbled, but he caught himself just in time. For a minute he stood still to catch his breath, his heart racing.

He went on, his mind still buzzing with the conversations of the morning. He thought of the young widow whose land had been seized by a greedy elder in her tribe. How she had wept! Right behind her had been the group from Hebron—their case had been blocked in the past by Absalom's schemes. After all these years, they had finally reached him today. How could he have neglected them so long? Their fathers had been good to him during his years in Hebron.

I need to mention that to Solomon as well. And urge him to remember the Lord's reputation. And remind him about the sons of Barzillai. And . . . There were so many things to remember.

David pushed through the door into the sunroom and hobbled to the window where he could let the sun shine full on his face. His bones ached, and his sides heaved. It was good that Solomon was taking over. The weight of the kingdom needed to rest on younger shoulders. Yet the responsibilities were so great. Was his son ready? Would Israel descend once more into disgrace and injustice, dragging the Lord's name down before the nations?

David picked up a well-worn harp and strummed the strings. There was only One with shoulders strong enough to bear such burdens. He had promised He would be with Solomon. And with Israel. Yes—God had promised! David would settle for nothing less.

Looking out over Jerusalem to the surrounding mountains and beyond, David lifted his heart in prayer. Relief washed over him as he brought the burdens one by one and left them with great anticipation before the Lord.

The Spirit guided him. He asked for the greatest blessings for his son that he could imagine—blessings that would bring peace and prosperity to the people and international glory to the Lord. Joy filled him as he imagined the wondrous works that only God could do, and he asked for them one after another. He envisioned the nation ruled with righteousness and cities overflowing with joyful people—people from all over the world blessing the God of Israel.

Soon his foot tapped with a tune inside him that just wouldn't let him hold still any longer. He thought of all the great promises God had made him in his youth. All the victories. The riches. The Lord had fulfilled all his desires until now and kept every promise.

And He will do even more for Solomon if I just ask Him.

His stiff legs couldn't carry him fast enough as he walked to his table and sat down heavily before a pile of scrolls. Shoving most of them aside, he seized a fresh piece of papyrus and scrawled in ink across the top "For Solomon."[1] Humming as he worked, he began putting his prayer in written form, this time organizing it into lines and stanzas.

He paused, considering. The envoys had spoken of Tarshish and other kingdoms—especially Sheba. The wealth of those distant lands still lay mostly beyond his reach—but not God's! He would include those in his prayer.

With a glowing heart and a prophetic eye, David imagined his future Heir—the ultimate Anointed One, the Messiah. He pulled out all the stops—asking for his nation to fear God forever, all kingdoms to serve the King, and eternal peace to prevail. Reaching the climax, with tears nearly choking him, he put the greatest longing of his heart into words once again.

"Blessed be the Lord, the God of Israel, who alone does wondrous things. . . . May the whole earth be filled with his glory! Amen and Amen!" (Ps. 72:18–19).

The Lord urges His people, "Open your mouth wide, and I will fill it" (Ps. 81:10). This prayer and its fulfillment are a terrific example of "opening wide." You can find the prayer written out in your Bible as Psalm 72. With this imaginative scene fresh in your mind, go ahead and read the entire psalm for yourself. I hope the words will stand out to you in a new way.

One thing you'll notice is that David does a lot of asking. There are at least nineteen requests and possibly quite a few more, depending on how you break them down. What stands out to me is how *big* the requests are and yet *specific* at the same time. This is a prayer that flows from a long life of practiced faith.

PSALM 72

¹ Give the king your justice, O God,
    and your righteousness to the royal son!
² May he judge your people with righteousness,
    and your poor with justice!
³ Let the mountains bear prosperity for the people,
    and the hills, in righteousness!

[4] May he defend the cause of the poor of the people,
    give deliverance to the children of the needy,
    and crush the oppressor!
[5] May they fear you while the sun endures,
    and as long as the moon, throughout all
    generations!
[6] May he be like rain that falls on the mown grass,
    like showers that water the earth!
[7] In his days may the righteous flourish,
    and peace abound, till the moon be no more!
[8] May he have dominion from sea to sea,
    and from the River to the ends of the earth!
[9] May desert tribes bow down before him,
    and his enemies lick the dust!
[10] May the kings of Tarshish and of the coastlands
    render him tribute;
    may the kings of Sheba and Seba bring gifts!
[11] May all kings fall down before him,
    all nations serve him!
[12] For he delivers the needy when he calls,
    the poor and him who has no helper.
[13] He has pity on the weak and the needy,
    and saves the lives of the needy.
[14] From oppression and violence he redeems their life,
    and precious is their blood in his sight.
[15] Long may he live;
    may gold of Sheba be given to him!
    May prayer be made for him continually,
    and blessings invoked for him all the day!

¹⁶ May there be abundance of grain in the land;
     on the tops of the mountains may it wave;
     may its fruit be like Lebanon;
     and may people blossom in the cities
     like the grass of the field!
¹⁷ May his name endure forever,
     his fame continue as long as the sun!
     May people be blessed in him,
     all nations call him blessed!
¹⁸ Blessed be the LORD, the God of Israel,
     who alone does wondrous things.
¹⁹ Blessed be his glorious name forever;
     may the whole earth be filled with his glory!
     Amen and Amen!
²⁰ The prayers of David, the son of Jesse, are
     ended.

Wondrous Things

Other than a couple of small sections, almost every line in this psalm is actually a request.[2] Did you notice how *big* many of these requests are? Though David was praying for Solomon, the blessing he sought included all of God's people in Israel (72:2–4), and "the poor" in particular (72:4, 12). Imagine asking God for enough food to satisfy your nation with plenty (72:3, 16) or peace for your country as long as the moon endures (72:7). That's some big praying!

Even more, David goes on to request vast territorial gains—to the full extent of what God had promised (72:8; see Exod. 23:31). He prays that *all* nations would serve his son (72:11) and again that *all* nations would "call him blessed" (72:17). When he reaches the climax, he prays, "May the whole earth be filled with [the Lord's] glory" (72:19). Is there anything bigger he could possibly ask for?

Notice that these requests aren't just vague, pie-in-the-sky wishes with no clear fulfillment, like the generic predictions in Chinese fortune cookies. David is very specific in what he asks for. He mentions "the River" as a definite boundary (72:8), a clear reference to the Euphrates. He also mentions Tarshish, Sheba, and Seba by name (72:10). He asks for long life for Solomon and very specifically for "gold of Sheba [to] be given to him" (72:15).

Was David just crazy and dreaming? Was he merely expressing patriotic sentiment or wishes from his fatherly heart without any real expectation of fulfillment? Or was he counting on God to take him seriously and answer his prayer on such a vast scale?

History confirms that God took him seriously. For one thing, He gave Solomon wisdom like no one else before or after him, specifically so he could "do justice" (1 Kings 3:28). This answer was even more than David had asked for (Ps. 72:1–2). God gave Solomon long life (1 Kings 11:42; Ps. 72:15) and incredible fame (1 Kings 4:31; 10:1; Ps. 72:17). In fact, his fame *did* "continue as long as the sun" (Ps. 72:17) because his story is recorded in the eternal Word of God. After all, here we are reading about Solomon three thousand years after his death!

The nation lived in happiness and prosperity (1 Kings 4:20, 25; Ps. 72:3, 7, 16). Foreign nations paid tribute to Solomon (1 Kings 4:21; Ps. 72:10) or brought gifts (1 Kings 10:24–25; Ps. 72:10). Even David's incredibly vast request that "all nations serve him" (Ps. 72:11) finds at least a partial fulfillment. "All the kingdoms from the Euphrates to the land of the Philistines and to the border of Egypt . . . served Solomon all the days of his life" (1 Kings 4:21).

The most outstanding example of God's answer in Solomon's day took place in the visit of the Queen of Sheba. In response to hearing of his fame, she came to investigate with hard questions, only to be utterly amazed in the end by what she saw. She gave Solomon a fortune in gold from Sheba (1 Kings 10:10), an incredibly specific point that David had prayed about (Ps. 72:15). Even more important, she exclaimed, "Blessed be the LORD your God" (1 Kings 10:9; Ps. 72:18).

In that statement you have the whole point—blessed be the Lord! All these glorious blessings for Solomon and Israel happened so that God would be glorified. Foreign nations praised the Lord's name. The poor in Israel could bless the Lord for His grace to them. Millennia later, the Lord is still receiving honor for what He did. David's prayer changed the whole nation and the world in ways that brought the biggest kind of honor and pleasure to God.

It gets even better! When David's ultimate heir, our Lord Jesus, reigns in peace over the entire earth from David's throne (Isa. 9:7), then we will see the fulfillment of this prayer to its fullest extent. The glory that God will receive cannot be imagined until then, and it will never end.

As we look at David's example, I want to invite you to consider a way of praying that might take you a bit beyond what you're used to. It fits what Christ taught us to ask: "Your kingdom come" (Matt. 6:10). It's the way of praying for God's will to be done on a large scale. God actually tells us in one place to pray "for all people" (1 Tim. 2:1). Such praying includes people and places you'll never see or touch yourself. Sometimes I ask the Lord to do "God-sized" things—works that are so big no one but God could do them.

Christ told the disciples, "If you abide in me, and my words abide in you, ask *whatever you wish*, and it will be done for you. *By this my Father is glorified*, that you bear much fruit and so prove to be my disciples" (John 15:7–8, emphasis added). When your basis is God's Word and your goal is spiritual fruit, you can be confident of answers to prayer that glorify God, even to the scope of "whatever you wish"!

How big are the Bible-based "whatevers" you're asking for? It's easy to complain about how bad things are in the world. What if we prayed about those matters instead? Rather than settling for "the way things are," let your love for Christ's glory move you to pray specific, big requests about the generation you live in. Make a difference!

Praying for Modern Sheba

Sometimes it helps to have an example, so let's take a significant need in our world today and see if we can apply this lesson about big, specific prayers for Christ's kingdom to that need.

I mentioned the nation of Yemen in chapter 3. This small country on the southwest corner of the Arabian Peninsula boasts a population nearly as large as Saudi Arabia's—more than 34 million and still growing. Yemen's territory is part of what used to be the kingdom of Sheba back in King David's day. In that era it was known for its wealth. Sadly, today the country is known for its suffering.

From 2014 until the time I'm writing (2024), the nation has been torn apart by a bloody civil war. News reports express the hopelessness that Yemenis feel. Children have lost limbs, family members, and even their lives. About 80 percent of the people depend on aid from outside the country to meet their basic needs. Many hospitals and schools have shut down. Sickness and starvation are claiming as many lives as bullets and bombs.

Even more urgent is Yemen's spiritual need. For almost fourteen hundred years, the religious scene has been dominated by Islam. Today well over 99 percent of the people are Muslim. Most have never seen a Bible or heard the gospel message.

So how can we pray for Yemen in such a way that God will be glorified?

If you heard this report in church and were asked to pray on the spot, it might be challenging. Perhaps you would talk to God about the facts of the case. You might repeat some of it back to Him. Not knowing what else to say—especially if you hadn't been able to prepare—you might follow with, "So please just be with them and help them," or something similar. I am certain God would know how to use your prayer.

But since the needs of Yemen are *big* and *specific*, I believe the Lord would be more glorified—whether you're praying publicly or alone—by big, specific requests. It takes time to think of them, but it can be eternally valuable to the people you're praying for. Consider a few possibilities.

1. **Provision**. Ask God to supply food, water, shelter, medicine, and education for the Yemeni people (Ps. 145:15–17; Matt. 5:45).
2. **Protection**. Ask God to guard the people from harm in body, mind, and soul. Ask God to prevent teenage boys and even younger ones from being drafted into the fighting. Ask for believers to be delivered from temptations and from evil people who would hinder them from following Christ (Ps. 121:8; 2 Thess. 3:2–3).
3. **Preachers**. Ask God to raise up a multitude of Yemeni believers who grow strong enough in the faith and in the Word to become spiritual leaders and witnesses of the gospel (2 Tim. 2:2; Eph. 4:11–12).

4. **Penetration**. Ask that the gospel message would spread to *every* tribe and even every individual in Yemen (2 Thess. 3:1; 1 Tim. 2:4).

It's no exaggeration to say that there are probably hundreds of other specific ways to pray for God to bless the Yemeni people. It takes some effort to dig into the details. It requires faith to pray in earnest for things that seem so impossible. But just think—if God answered even these four requests by themselves, millions of lives could be changed!

Challenges to Praying Big

God's call for us to open our mouths wide (Ps. 81:10) is an amazing offer! It helps to realize, though, that this kind of praying involves some challenges. One of the most daunting of those challenges is *fear*. If you're praying with others, you might worry that they'll think you're unrealistic. Or worse—what if you publicly ask for something specific, and it doesn't happen? Then everyone might notice.

Even if you're praying alone, it can be frightening to ask for something that is humanly impossible. You know God *can* do it in theory, but it still might feel overwhelming. You don't want to get your hopes up only to have them dashed if God doesn't do what you ask Him. It feels a lot safer to stick with indefinite prayers—like "please be with them"—because you won't be disappointed with a lack of results. A major downside is that you miss out on the joy of seeing God answer in specific ways.

Christ taught that fear stems from having "little faith" (Matt. 8:26). Suppose, for instance, you want your church to organize a mission trip to West Africa, but you're afraid it's too unrealistic to ask God about it. That fear may be the dashboard light reflecting a *faith* issue under the hood.

The answer to overcoming fear and faith issues is to spend more time in God's faith-building Word. See for yourself how passionate God is about His work in the whole world. Let the Scriptures be your source of ideas for what to ask; you can be sure God is eager to do the things He talks about. Meditating on God's answers to David and others or memorizing God's promises can be wonderful boosts to faith-filled praying. The same God who ruled the nations in the past is still on the highest throne today.

Perhaps the main challenge to big praying, however, is simply *selfishness*. When it comes right down to it, we find it easier to pray vague prayers. It takes a few seconds to say, "Please be with the missionary family in Cambodia." But to pray specifically about that family's health, the children's schooling, the weather, safety, their personal devotions, open hearts in an upcoming outreach, and restoration for an estranged believer in the church—that kind of praying takes a lot more effort.

It's a heavy burden to carry perishing souls to the throne of God. When we're tired (or even when we're not), lighter activities like a sports game, a work project, or an engrossing book can have more appeal than laboring in intercession for the nations. But here's the good news—we're not alone in carrying that burden. The Holy Spirit comes alongside us to help us pray (Rom. 8:26–27). Even if our bodies and minds feel faint, we can be assured that when we make the sacrifice to pray, our Father will see and respond (Matt. 6:6). God's presence is enough for us to overcome the challenges.

Growing into Praying Big

If you're willing to overcome the obstacles, how do you learn to pray God-glorifying prayers like David's?

First, begin with small steps of faith, based on where you are. Big praying requires big faith. But how do you get there? One step at a time. The initial step might be a specific prayer for God to help you share a gospel tract. Next it might be the act of sharing the tract with a cashier when God opens the opportunity. Then later you can ask God to give you an opportunity to follow up on that cashier, and watch what He does. Each answered prayer and act of obedience will grow your faith to ask God for even more.

David was probably near the end of his days by the time he prayed Psalm 72 (not that you should wait that long). He'd had a whole lifetime full of faith-building experiences. At times, he despaired of God coming through for him (1 Sam. 27:1), but the Lord proved His faithfulness every time (1 Kings 1:29). The victories over lions and bears gave him courage to take on giants and then enemy kingdoms. Those victories gave him faith for even bigger answers to prayer.

But how do you know where to start or what step to take next? The second key to growth in prayer is learning to listen to God. He shows the steps of faith to the ones who listen.

David was a man who knew how to listen to God. His greatest prayers were responses to what God had first said to him (see 2 Samuel 7, for example). He wrote about God speaking to him and his heart responding (Ps. 27:8). He counted on God to teach him and direct his steps (Ps. 25:4–5, 12). Before making big decisions, he asked God for counsel and then acted on what God said (1 Sam. 30:8; 2 Sam. 5:19). When he prayed Psalm 72, we can be certain he wasn't just wishing randomly. He was led by the Spirit and the specific promises God had given him.

Of course, David was led in unique ways because God had made a covenant with him that included specific promises (2 Sam. 7:12–16), and the Holy Spirit was guiding him to write inspired Scripture. But we can be just as certain of God directing us in our prayers as David was. The Spirit of Christ teaches us what Christ wants us to know (John 16:12–15; 1 Cor. 2:12–16) and helps us when we're not sure what to pray (Rom. 8:26–27). He is our Teacher to direct us what to ask for. Do we pay attention to Him or just rattle off prepackaged requests?

You may have noticed in the example prayers for Yemen that I included verse references after each request. The Bible is the primary source for knowing God's heart about a matter so we can pray according to His will. I find that the prayers that most move my heart and embolden my faith are ones triggered by my Teacher using specific verses (John 15:7).

Let me offer you this challenge:

Begin each daily prayer time by asking the Lord, "What do You want me to pray for?" Then be attentive to the Scriptures and ideas that He brings to mind.

I wonder how much God would do if we learned to pray according to His leading. The zeal of the Lord is great (Isa. 9:7; 37:32), and if we slowed down enough to let Him guide us, we might pray for things far bigger than we originally planned to. In my imagination, I picture the needs of our world spread out like the vast, scorching sands of the great Sahara Desert. Just above that God holds out grace the size of the Mediterranean Sea, ready to flood every inch of that desert. But the primary channel He has chosen for the water to flow through is prayer, and too often we offer a mere coffee straw!

Ponder the scope of God's plan expressed in Isaiah 49. He promised Christ that He would use Him to do the impossible—to restore the rebellious tribes of Israel to fellowship with their Lord and with each other.

Considering their history, such an accomplishment would be an absolute marvel! It took the death and resurrection of God's Son to make it possible. But then the Father says of that monumental task of restoring Israel, "It is too light a thing." Too light? Yes, those are His words. The Father explains how He will do an even greater work: "I will make you as a light for the nations, that my salvation may reach to the end of the earth" (Isa. 49:6).

David's prayers tied into God's ultimate plan in Christ, and ours can as well. Nothing is too hard for God (Jer. 32:17). No honor is so high that Christ would be unworthy of it (Rev. 5:9–12). For His sake, will you join with David in praying for Christ's glory to spread universally? Will you take steps of growth in praying big, specific prayers for our generation? We have a great God who has given us great promises, and He is willing to do great things for His Son.

Dear Father, You made the universe. You rule the nations and write the pages of history. I am sorry for restricting my prayers so often when Your Son is worthy of so much glory. Please show me Your heart for the people around me and teach me to recognize Your prompting in my spirit so I can pray for them according to Your zeal. Please teach our generation to pray in bold faith and grant us an awakening bigger than ever before. I surrender my time and my will to be led in praying big, specific prayers because You love me, and I love You. In Jesus's name, amen.

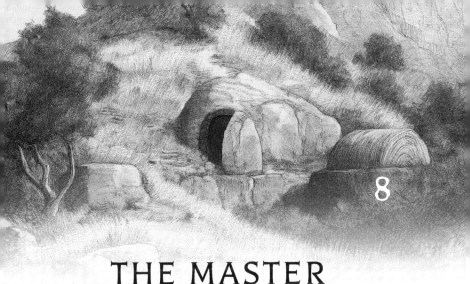

THE MASTER EXAMPLE

THE LORD JESUS

JOHN 11:1–45

The Lord Jesus was still at a distance from Lazarus's house when He saw Martha, one of Lazarus's sisters, rushing up the path toward Him. Her head was down, and she held a hand over her mouth. He stood still, waiting for her to reach Him. Hot rays of sun sent streams of sweat running through His hair.

Behind Him, in the near silence, He could hear the crunch of footsteps as His twelve men came up and stood waiting behind Him. He could hear a couple of them speaking in hushed tones. They had risked their lives coming with Him back into

Judea despite the Jewish leaders' threats. It was good they had come. They didn't realize yet how much they needed the lesson He was about to teach them—or how much the teaching affected Him emotionally.

As Martha approached, she brushed a loose strand of graying hair back from her face. Her shoulders sagged, and large, dark circles stood out beneath her eyes. How grief had changed her complexion!

"Lord," she said in a hoarse voice. "If You had been here, my brother would not have died." She searched His face. The words were a question as much as a statement. Why hadn't He come earlier? Why had He let Lazarus die?

A lump formed in Jesus's throat. The Father had already revealed to Him that His friend was dead. But to hear the actual words and see the pain this meant for Martha . . .

She straightened a little and wiped her sleeve across her face. "But even now I know that whatever You ask from God, God will give You."

She had said it. The issue was out in the open—could Jesus truly get *anything* He wanted by asking the Father? This unexpected death had aroused some of the darkest doubts a person could face. Martha and Mary had brought Lazarus's need to the Lord—and still their brother had died. Why?

Martha had been well chosen for this trial. What faith she expressed! But He could see in her eyes that she was shaken. The disciples behind Him would be even more shaken within a short time as they watched Him die on the cross. It was time to strengthen them.

"Your brother will rise again."

Jesus comforted Martha, assuring her that He Himself was the resurrection and the life. Soon after, He comforted Mary as well. They brought Him with a crowd of their friends to see the grave, and He wept with them. He couldn't help it. His heart ached at the weight of their grief, and even more because He knew He could have prevented it. But this had to be done, and when the lesson was over, their joy would be eternal.

At His command, several men with puzzled expressions removed the stone from the mouth of the cave where Lazarus was buried. The dark hole lay open to the sun, and everyone stared into it, seeing nothing. Then Jesus saw the eyes turning back toward Him. This was the moment.

He lifted His eyes and stared into the blue heavens. He could imagine the Father leaning forward and listening. There was no question about Lazarus's resurrection. That had been settled days ago when Jesus first learned of the sickness and spent the evening in earnest prayer. God had already answered, and all that remained now was to carry it out.

But the lesson needed to be given.

"Father," Jesus prayed, loud enough for all around Him to hear the words. "I thank You that You have heard Me. I knew that You always hear Me, but I said this on account of the people standing around, that they may believe that You sent Me."

Then with joy He turned His face toward that dark hole once more. "Lazarus," He called, "come out!"

Silence hung in the air as each onlooker held his breath. Then an excited shriek burst from Mary, and in a second the whole crowd erupted as Jesus's friend shuffled out of the cave into the light, still wrapped in strips of white cloth.

"Unbind him, and let him go," Jesus said. Men jumped to obey, no more questions in their eyes now. They kept looking back at Him with expressions of awe that couldn't be hidden. They believed Him.

John, one of the twelve, came up and held His arm. Jesus could feel him trembling.

"He came back to life, Lord. God heard You, just like Martha said—and You said!"

"Yes, John." And the Father would hear the disciples as well. Jesus would be with them only a short time more. Soon it would be their turn.

"The Father sent Me." He put His arm around John's shoulders. "He always hears Me."

Christ's words to the Father in John 11:42, "You always hear me," give us a unique window into our Lord's prayer life. He knew that He had come from the Father to accomplish a specific mission. And He knew that to accomplish that mission He could ask for whatever He needed—and the Father would do it. Every time.

Not long after this climactic demonstration, Christ taught His disciples that soon He would return to the

Father and send them out to carry on His mission. They—
and now we—could count on success by the very same
principle. "If you ask me anything in my name," He said,
"I will do it" (John 14:14). Then later, "Whatever you ask
of the Father in my name, he will give it to you" (16:23).

Our mission to do Christ's works by prayer parallels
His life of doing the Father's works by prayer. So as we seek
to grow in prayer, what better way could we find than
examining the prayer life of Christ Himself? He is our
ultimate example—the Master—the One we have committed to follow.

A thorough study of Christ's prayer life would require
a lengthy tome if not several volumes. Such a study goes
far beyond my goal here. In this chapter, I'd like to cap-
ture just three key matters that Christ focused His
prayers on: personal victory, powerful ministry, and people He loved. As we observe Him in each case, we can
evaluate our own prayer lives by comparison.

Don't be discouraged by Christ's perfection. Even
though He was God, He was also completely man, and
He experienced the same temptations and limitations
that we do (Heb. 4:15). He has called us to follow Him
(John 12:26), and even though we don't do it perfectly,
it's our job as His disciples to copy His example (1 John
2:6; 1 Pet. 2:21).

In the next chapter, we'll return to studying Abraham so we can find hope for ourselves as struggling
prayer warriors—what God can do in spite of our weakness. For now, let's set our gaze on Christ so we can

be changed to be more like Him (2 Cor. 3:18). Also remember that Christ Himself lives in you by His Spirit if you are one of His, and He can empower you from within to pray as He prayed.

Prayer for Personal Victory

On the darkest night of His life, as Jesus anticipated His impending death the next day, He went out into the Garden of Gethsemane to seek the Father. He urged His disciples to "watch and pray" so they wouldn't cave in to the great temptations that would soon overtake them (Matt. 26:41). Sadly, the disciples failed to heed the warning. Overcome with sorrow, they fell asleep.

Poor Peter. He had a tremendous desire to serve the Lord. He was willing to lay down his life for Christ. He even jumped forward all by himself to attack the soldiers who came to arrest his Master. But for all his good intentions he succumbed to fear and absolutely failed on that night of temptation. How different his story might have been if only he had prepared himself in prayer as Jesus had urged him.

How different our stories might have been too, in many cases, if we had been on guard and prayed.

By contrast, the Lord Jesus succeeded where Peter and we have failed. On the night above all nights when His body needed a good rest, He gave up that rest in order to seek the Father. He was following His own counsel to Peter and persevering in prayer so that He wouldn't fall to temptation. He knew He could never make it through the shame and scourging the next day—let alone the crucifixion—apart from divine grace.

How did He get that grace? By persevering in prayer for it.

Think what He endured the next day! He was falsely accused. He was spit on. He was humiliated before a host of pagan soldiers. He was betrayed by His own people. He was torn to shreds by a whipping that could have killed Him. He had long thorns beaten into His head. Then while every fiber of His body cried out for relief, He was forced to carry a massive crossbeam to His own execution until He couldn't take another step and had to be given help.

A further detail in this scene moves me more than almost any other: "They offered him wine mixed with myrrh, but he did not take it" (Mark 15:23). They offered Him relief from the pain right before the crucifixion, and He turned it down flat. Think how many excuses He could have made to justify taking that small relief: *this might reenergize Me; it won't hinder My focus; Proverbs even says to give wine to someone who is dying!*

But Christ would not give up control of His mind or heart in even the smallest way. He willingly experienced every ounce of torture the cross could give Him. Where did He find the inner strength and discernment to endure so much when His body and spirit were exhausted beyond imagination?

Christ had obtained that strength in advance. He'd received it as a gift from His Father in the hours of prayer the night before in Gethsemane. Because He watched and prayed, He was prepared to endure death itself, "even death on a cross" (Phil. 2:8).

Consider that prayer. He began by expressing honestly His feelings and His need. "Abba, Father, all things are possible for you. Remove this cup from me" (Mark 14:36). This was no formal petition—He cried out in agony about how much He hurt. He knew that the cup wouldn't be removed. But the expression of human neediness must have drawn out His Father's stores of compassion and grace like nothing else could. Then Christ submitted His will to the Father: "Yet not what I will, but what you will." He is our example. We also ought to be bold in expressing our personal feelings and need for grace. Then we ought to submit to God's best plan for responding to us.

Praying about ongoing trials or impending temptation requires perseverance. We read that after seeking to arouse the sleeping disciples, Christ went back for a second and later a third round of prayer, "saying the same words" (Mark 14:39). There was a burden on His heart that couldn't be immediately relieved. He had to keep on praying until He'd gotten the peace from God that surpasses understanding. Then He was ready.

What trials or temptations are you facing? Maybe you're heading into a workday among foul-mouthed coworkers. Perhaps you're worried about giving in to anger at your children—again. Maybe you're facing another round of media fire against your ministry's stance on morality. Or are you facing danger because of witnessing in a hostile environment?

Whatever your personal scenario, Christ's message and example still apply. "Watch and pray." Prepare in advance—perhaps first thing each day—by taking time with God. Express your weakness and your need for grace. Wait before the Lord if necessary to let Him assure you of receiving that promised grace.

If you're one of Christ's, then His Spirit lives inside you (Rom. 8:9). He will help you pray and obtain the strength you need for personal victory.

Prayer for Powerful Ministry

In the account of Lazarus's resurrection in John 11, we get a glimpse into another key focus of Christ's praying: He prayed about His works. In fact, that's how He did His works. Prayer was His regular mode of operation for doing ministry.

The Gospels don't often record that Christ prayed before miracles—probably because He prayed silently. But people knew what was going on. The blind man that Christ healed in John 9 explained the miracle this way: "Why, this is an amazing thing! You do not know where [Jesus] comes from, and yet he opened my eyes. We know that God does not listen to sinners, but if anyone is a worshiper of God and does his will, *God listens to him*" (9:30-31, emphasis added).

Martha emphasized the same point in speaking to Jesus: "Whatever you ask from God, God will give you" (John 11:22). Our Lord verified her words by His public prayer to the Father, "I knew that you always hear me" (11:42). Though He was the One who commanded Lazarus to rise, He viewed what happened next not as coming from Himself—at least not from His human ability—but as an answer to His prayer.

"The Son can do nothing of his own accord," Christ said, "but only what he sees the Father doing. For whatever the Father does, that the Son does likewise" (5:19). Christ's dependence on the Father to do the works—the Father's works—is a major theme throughout the book of John. He says that the Father gave Him those works to do (5:36). It was also the Father who gave Him the words to speak—perhaps an even more significant aspect of His ministry work (12:49).

Think of Christ's ministry. He cast out demons. He opened blind eyes. He made deaf people hear. He calmed storms. He fed thousands of people out of just a handful of bread and fish. He proclaimed the good news to the poor in cities and villages all across the country. He taught the Scriptures like no one else. He transformed people's lives. How did He do it?

Here is His answer to the disciples: "The Father who dwells in me does his works" (14:10). Christ lived a life of dependence on the Father to work through Him.

Practically, that meant living a life of prayer. If necessary, He would rise to pray while it was still dark (Mark 1:35). Or He would stay up late on a remote mountainside to spend hours in prayer (Matt. 14:22–25). Despite carrying more responsibility than anyone in history, *He always found a way to make time for prayer.*[1]

How much do you pray about the work God gives you? We all probably remember to pray about "big" opportunities, such as special speaking engagements or mission trips. But we can involve God and His power in so many other ways!

We can ask God to sanctify our families through dinner conversations as well as family devotions. We can ask for chances to witness as we head to soccer games, business meetings, or medical appointments. We can pray over the multiple facets of our secular work projects or babysitting agendas. We can take our biggest, dearest dreams of how we'd love to serve Christ and talk about them openly with Him. Don't just wish. *Ask.*

As you follow your Master and yield to His guidance, you'll probably find out that He's not in as big a rush as you are. While the clock seems to shout, "Hurry! Hurry! Hurry!" in your mind, His still small voice will say, "In quietness and in trust shall be your strength" (Isa. 30:15). Your ministry won't be powerful because of all your efforts. When you experience God's power, it will happen for you as it happened for Jesus—as an answer to your time in prayer.

Prayer for People He Loved

Our Lord Jesus was a master intercessor, praying for His friends. When He told Peter that Satan wanted to sift him and the other disciples like wheat, He added, "But I have prayed for you that your faith may not fail. And when you have turned again, strengthen your brothers" (Luke 22:32). He didn't say "if you turn again" but "*when* you have turned again." He knew the Father would answer Him.

Christ prayed not only for Peter but for all the disciples. We have the privilege of reading at length one such prayer, recorded in John 17. Christ prayed specifically for the Father to keep the disciples faithful to Him, to sanctify them, and to unify them. Even more, He clarified that His prayer wasn't for those early disciples alone but also for us who would later believe in Him through the gospel (17:20).

Peter's testimony is perhaps one of the greatest turnarounds in all of history. He and the other apostles (minus Judas) stayed faithful to Christ and changed the world in their generation. For them and for us, salvation, sanctification, and union as God's children are all 100 percent guaranteed if we believe in Christ. Why? *Because Christ prayed.*

And His prayer life didn't end when He ascended to the Father. His work of intercession for us as our great high priest is happening right now. The book of Hebrews tells us that He "always lives" to intercede for us (7:25).

He keeps on praying for us. In fact, His intercessory work is so important that He left the world for the present time to stay at the Father's right hand in His priestly role on our behalf.

There is much we don't know about how Christ intercedes or what He asks for us as individuals. But whatever grace you're experiencing in your life right now, you can probably attribute that to Christ's work of praying for you. Even when you greatly disappoint Him, as Peter did, you can hear Him say, "But I have prayed for you."

As you grow in your relationship with the Lord Jesus, He will develop in you this heart to pray for others as well. Though He alone is the *high* priest, we also are part of a "holy priesthood" (1 Pet. 2:5), bringing the needs of our generation before God. Paul is an excellent example of following Christ in this regard. He told Timothy, "I remember you constantly in my prayers night and day" (2 Tim. 1:3). He prayed faithfully for the churches as well (Rom. 1:9–10; Eph. 1:16; Phil. 1:4; Col. 1:3; 1 Thess. 1:2; 3:10; 2 Thess. 1:11).

I have a memory from my university days of my friend Alex carrying scraps of paper in his shirt pocket. Whenever we would see each other, he'd ask me, "How can I pray for you?" Then he'd write down my requests on one of those scraps—squished in among requests from so many others. Only the Lord knows how many lives—like mine— have been changed by faithful friends who imitate Christ's prayer life.

Let me offer you an exercise that I think can help you take another step in following Christ. In this brief chapter, we've studied how He prayed for personal victory, for power in ministry, and for the people He loved.

> List these three areas of prayer in order from your strongest one to your weakest one. For the next month, ask God every day to grow you to be more like Christ in that area where you are weakest. "Lord, teach me to pray."

Of course, you can pray about the stronger areas as well. When I evaluated myself, I saw some weaknesses in every one of the three areas.

The disciples asked Christ to teach them to pray because they were moved by His example (Luke 11:1). They definitely needed to be taught! When a father brought his demon-possessed son to them, they failed to cast it out because of their small faith and lack of prayer (Matt. 17:20; Mark 9:29). At times, instead of interceding, they were quick to turn away people, like little children or a persistent foreign woman who was trying to get help (Luke 18:15–16; Matt. 15:22–23). One time His disciples asked for fire from heaven rather than grace (Luke 9:54). While Christ labored in prayer in Gethsemane, they fell asleep and later caved to temptation.

But Christ succeeded in teaching them. When we read the book of Acts, we find them praying together frequently with unified hearts and minds (1:14, 24; 2:42; 4:24; 12:5, 12). In fact, when faced with overwhelming responsibilities, they imitated their Master's example of keeping prayer and the ministry of the Word as their top priorities (6:4). God blessed the apostles' prayer life with an impact that reaches our lives even today.

The Lord loves you and is ready to teach you to pray as well. It takes time. But He's praying for you. You can be confident that He will succeed if you're willing to learn.

Lord Jesus, I praise You for Your perfect example. You never felt guilty, like we do, about shortcomings in Your prayer life. Thank You for teaching so much in Your Word about prayer, and I ask You to train me personally to pray as You prayed. I believe You live in me, and I ask You to direct me from within so that I pray according to Your will and power, by Your Spirit. The world needed men like the eleven disciples and then Paul in their day who had learned to pray. Please raise up such men and women of prayer in our generation and make me one of them. May the Father be glorified in the Son and in His people. Amen.

9

WHEN GOD
SAYS NO

ABRAHAM

GENESIS 19:23–29

Dew soaked Abraham's sandals as he raced up the grassy sheep track to the top of the final rise. The crisp morning was so quiet it seemed to be holding its breath. Abraham's sides heaved, and he slowed his pace but kept on walking. He couldn't take the suspense any longer!

All night he had tossed and turned, wondering how the Lord would respond to his prayer. Would the Lord spare Sodom after all? Would He find ten righteous people there? Would Abraham's nephew Lot and his family survive?

He tried to push thoughts of the other possibility out of his mind, but his hopes were growing thinner with each step. The gray sky seemed hazier than usual in the distance. Now he was almost to the overlook where he had met with the Lord the day before and begged Him to spare the city.

As he crested the grassy rise, the valley suddenly came into view. His heart sank into his stomach at the sight, and a groan escaped him. What had once been a lush, verdant grassland now appeared to be a charred, barren wilderness. Smoke ascended from every corner. Through the haze he saw the smoldering wreck that had once been the great city of Sodom.

Flames still flickered above the blackened buildings. Even as Abraham watched, one of the towers tilted and then sank into a plume of dark smoke. The noise of crashing stones echoed from the valley into the mountains.

Abraham's eyes might have been playing tricks on him, but he thought he could make out tiny black dots—the dead bodies of men, women, and even children. Were any of them his family members? He thought of their faces. He thought of the people of Sodom he had rescued from the enemy kings. Now he stood looking out over their destruction. Surely not a soul had survived such a blow.

The wind shifted, and smoke wafted past him, stinging his eyes. A foul odor engulfed his nostrils, and he nearly doubled over, holding his face in his long sleeve as a shield. The smell of burning sulfur was worse than rotten eggs—the stench of judgment and death.

Abraham rushed back the way he had come. He wandered for a time, weaving between rocks and scraggly trees, trying to clear his lungs—and even more his mind—from smoke.

How could this have happened? He'd poured so much of his life into Lot. When they had parted ways, he'd never guessed that things would go this far. But hadn't he done the right thing? Hadn't he prayed? Hadn't God sent him to rescue Sodom all those years ago? Why? Why would he go to all those efforts only for this?

He sank onto his knees in the grass and sighed. Then he lifted his eyes and searched the sky. What was God doing?

Abraham had drawn near to the Lord and poured out his heart. He'd done everything he could. What had he gotten for all his pain? He hung his head.

As far as he could see with his eyes, all he'd gotten was a face full of smoke.

Have you ever had an experience like that?

Genesis 19:27–28 says, "Abraham went early in the morning to the place where he had stood before the LORD. And he looked down toward Sodom and Gomorrah and toward all the land of the valley, and he looked and, behold, the smoke of the land went up like the smoke of a furnace."

Can you imagine how Abraham must have felt? I've tried to envision the scene and describe it above. We know that Abraham didn't lose his faith. But he surely must have hurt.

Take careful note of the specific request that he had prayed the day before for Sodom. He requested that God spare the city (Gen. 18:24). The Lord responded that if He found enough righteous people there, He would "spare the whole place" (18:26). In Abraham's mind, the issue was Sodom's survival—that's what he was begging for. It's hard to imagine receiving a louder answer of no than what Abraham saw that morning as he stared out over the smoldering ruins.

Most likely, you too have experienced God answering no—or at least answers that felt like no. I certainly have. Sometimes a no hurts more than other times. I remember a grieving couple who shared with me their experience of losing an adult child. In conclusion the wife said, "I'm sure the Lord answers other people's prayers. But not ours."

You may not be able to identify in your own life such a significant disappointment as theirs, but perhaps you can think of other instances when it didn't appear that God answered you—prayers for a parent to attend church, for a loved one to recover, or for an employer to give you a raise. Then there are the prayers you pray regularly for a good day or for victory in your own life or another's, only to see no apparent difference in the outcome.

Experiencing such disappointments can take a huge toll on your prayer life if you aren't alert to the danger. After getting a face full of smoke, you may say things to yourself such as "Why try so hard anymore?" "What difference are my prayers making anyway?" "Maybe intercession works for real prayer warriors, but I don't have the faith for it." "God is going to do whatever His will is anyway, so what difference does praying make?"

Maybe you would never say such things out loud because you would immediately recognize them as false if you voiced them. But deep down inside, your faith takes a blow—or is chipped away little by little.

Even after that, I'm sure you would still pray. You know it's the right thing to do. You would probably still expect the Lord to answer sometimes. But as you consider your prayer life right now, have you lost the zeal you once had? Have you settled for saying prayers without expecting much as a result? Have you drawn back from fasting and crying so you won't hurt so much—just in case? Have you chosen to limit yourself to small, manageable prayers? Is there a certain type of praying or an area of prayer you just stay away from?

I believe our experiences of receiving negative answers may be one of the biggest challenges we face in our prayer lives. We could avoid the issue and focus only on the glorious yes answers. Those are faith strengthening. But I think if we could come to grips with what God does through the no answers, our faith would be strengthened even more. You may even get such a foothold here that you'll advance in prayer like never before. So let's see what the Bible says.

First of all, as the healed blind man said, "We know that God does not listen to sinners" (John 9:31). Often the Lord shows grace by hearing unsaved people, like the sailors on Jonah's escape ship (Jon. 1:14–15). But God is not obligated to answer them. If anyone prays with sin in his heart, he shouldn't expect an answer (Ps. 66:18; Isa. 59:1–2). If you pray for things that fuel your selfish ambitions, don't expect God to support such an agenda (James 4:3). Before proceeding, check to make sure you're praying with a clean heart.

Second, what sounds like "no" could end up being "wait." No doubt at some point Zechariah and Elizabeth felt that God had told them no about having a child. But it turned out that God was saying yes! They just needed to be patient.

However, sometimes there's no mistaking a definite no from the Lord—even when our hearts have been clean and it seems like we've done everything right. Consider Abraham's prayer for Sodom. He had drawn near to the Lord. He'd poured out his heart with genuine emotion. He'd expressed tremendous faith and love. He had persevered—keeping the request before the Lord repeatedly. He had watched expectantly. He had opened his mouth wide!

But only smoke.

What about those kinds of results? Let's survey three big reasons God sometimes says no to His faithful servants—and why we can even be glad He does.

God's Plan Is Better

There's a lot of overlap between these reasons, and in most cases all three are at work at once. Running through each of them is the same fundamental point—God often says no because He has something way better in mind.

Parents do the same thing on a regular basis. Imagine a little boy named Billy dashing into the kitchen with his cowboy hat on and a plastic shovel in his hand. He shouts, "Can I play in the dirt pile?" His mother says with a grin, "Not now. We're heading to the park for pizza with Grandma." I can imagine—if Billy is like my kids—that he would greet that no by singing the Hallelujah Chorus as he throws his hat high in the air and takes off to spread the news.

Perhaps if we knew our Father better, we would also rejoice more when He tells us no, even though the reason isn't as apparent as a picnic in the park.

Suppose God were always forced to give us what we ask for. We'd be in huge trouble. Once, when the people of Israel complained about having no meat, the Lord "gave them what they asked, but sent a wasting disease among them" (Ps. 106:15). Be careful about what you ask!

It is to our advantage that God reserves the right to say, "No, I have something far better for you."

One time a friend and I planned a survey trip to several countries in the Middle East. One leg of the trip had to be purchased through a travel agent in another country. He couldn't seem to understand our situation, and his lack of communication caused me a great deal of discomfort. I prayed for several weeks that he would get the issue resolved. I wrote to him in English with no success. I prayed some more. I wrote to him in Arabic and got a little further, but still no success. I kept praying. Finally, he said, "I'm sorry. Those tickets are no longer available. But I could get you some tickets for the week prior."

With a sigh, I agreed. I decided that the plans could be rearranged to put that part of the trip first. Then everything suddenly fell into place. As it turned out, the new travel plans accomplished our goal far better. By the time we were halfway through our trip, I couldn't help but see that God had directed the whole situation. As our plane headed for the next stop, I silently prayed, "Thank you, Lord, for saying no."

God Prioritizes Eternal Values

Again, imagine Billy asking his mother, "Can I go play in the dirt pile now?" This time she says, "Sorry. You're behind on your chores. Get your work done first, and then you can play if there's time." Why doesn't she just say yes right away? She (wisely) values her son's work ethic and character more than she values his immediate fun.

Our heavenly Father is even wiser in dealing with us than human parents are in dealing with their children. Often we come to Him focused on something we want, and He sees that something far more important is at stake.

For one thing, He puts a higher priority on our spiritual growth than on our immediate comfort. He may deny your prayers for relief from chastening because He's using the pain to produce in you "the peaceful fruit of righteousness" (Heb. 12:11).

Sometimes He uses testing in order to grow our faith. Paul tells about a problem that hurt him so much he called it "a messenger of Satan." He begged God three times to take it away. Instead, God said, "No, your weakness gives me the chance to display my power." Paul allowed God to realign his values— so much that he could even take pleasure in his own weakness! God's saying no to him made him a stronger follower of Christ (2 Cor. 12:7-10).

God also values what will build His eternal kingdom (and He knows that once we get there, we will value it as much as He does). Paul wrote, "This light momentary affliction is preparing for us an eternal weight of glory beyond all comparison" (2 Cor. 4:17). Sometimes the things we pray for may not fit in with God's plans to advance the gospel. Thankfully, He can say no.

I still remember one of my professors talking about how he (and many others) had prayed earnestly for God to heal Christian songwriter Ron Hamilton from cancer in his eye. But God said no, and Ron had to wear a patch over that eye socket for the rest of his life. As a result, though, he got a new nickname—Patch the Pirate—and began a musical ministry that has impacted millions of children (and adults). In hindsight my professor chuckled and said, "Wow. What a dumb prayer!"

Of course, it wasn't dumb at the time. God just had a better plan in mind. And even though you may not know why He hasn't resolved your court case or provided the new equipment for your church or restored your mother to you or made your terrifying memories go away, you can trust Him as your wise and loving Father.

Someday you may say something like my own mother said: "I didn't like having cancer. But if I had to go through it again, I would because of the closer relationship I enjoy with the Lord now."

God Knows What We Do Not Know

Once more imagine Billy asking, "Can I play in the dirt *now*?" His mother dries her hands on her apron and sighs. "I'm sorry, Billy. I can't explain why, but I can't let you play outside right now. Can you trust me?"

Maybe there's a surprise birthday present in the backyard (a giant toy excavator!). Or perhaps she's heard that a child predator escaped from the local jail. Her decision could be based on a message from the doctor that she isn't ready to share with Billy just yet. There are many possibilities. But the fact is, sometimes parents have to say no without being able to explain why.

Sometimes God has to do the same thing with us. Can you trust Him?

There's a lot that God knows and accounts for that we can't begin to know or understand. We don't know the past except for little pieces, and we don't fully understand how it connects to the current situation. We know only a little segment of the present condition of the world, our home, and even our own hearts. We can't understand—despite many attempts—how God gives us free choice and yet still works out His sovereign will.

We also don't know the future. But God does. Amy Carmichael, as a little child, asked the Lord to change her brown eyes to blue, but the Lord said no. She had no idea at the time that her brown eyes would be vital later for her disguise as a missionary rescuing children in India from slavery in the temples. But God saw the whole thing in advance. She came to be glad in the long run for His graciously saying no.

One aspect of what we don't know is harder to swallow but necessary to consider: we don't have all the necessary information to make perfect judgments. Sometimes it seems to us—like it did to Habakkuk—that God is idly letting sinners get away with their evil (Hab. 1:3) or, on the other hand, is being too harsh (1:17). But God knows when to show mercy and when to condemn. He knows people's motives. He knows what goes on in secret. He also knows how to be patient in His work of redemption.

Abraham might have wondered why God destroyed all the people in Sodom despite his heartfelt intercession. But ultimately, in the aftermath, he had to trust what he had prayed at the outset: "Shall not the Judge of all the earth do what is just?" (Gen. 18:25). The reasons God had for sparing Sodom in years past and destroying them later were known only to Him.

There was something else Abraham didn't know at the time, but God has chosen to reveal it to us. (This is where the story gets really good.) In the divine record we read, "So it was that, when God destroyed the cities of the valley, God remembered Abraham and sent Lot out of the midst of the overthrow" (Gen. 19:29). Based on the wording of this verse, it's my conviction that God showed mercy to Lot and his daughters not for their own sakes but because of Abraham's prayer. Abraham's "failed" prayer had made an impact after all.

The quality of the impact may seem questionable from the immediate context. The rest of the chapter explains that Lot went on to live in a cave with his daughters who later got him drunk and had children from him. Their descendants became the nations of Ammon and Moab, long-term enemies of the people of Israel. Not exactly a happily-ever-after ending.

But with God, there's always more to the story. He can take a failed prayer and make it into a blessing far bigger than anything you could ever imagine. For one thing, today

I have friends—dear brothers in Christ—from the region where Ammon and Moab lived. Who knows how many of them—not to mention any number of people throughout the world (maybe even you!)—descended from those two boys. Many souls will be singing and praising God forever in Christ's kingdom because God chose to remember Abraham's prayer.

Then consider what we discover as we follow God's story through the pages of Scripture. In the book of Ruth, we find a glorious redemption story of a foreigner who left her home to follow the true God. Where did she come from? Moab! I can't help but think that Ruth descended from the original Moab, and that means she wouldn't have existed apart from Abraham's "failed" prayer for the city of Sodom.

Go a little further. Ruth went on to marry Boaz, and as the story unfolds, they became the great-grandparents of David (Ruth 4:21–22). *The* David. The one who wrote most of the psalms. The one who prophesied about Christ. The one who became the great king of all Israel and the father of the whole Davidic dynasty! That whole line of kings might never have happened apart from Abraham's "failed" prayer.

Flip to the New Testament. "The book of the genealogy of Jesus Christ, the son of David, the son of Abraham" (Matt. 1:1). Our Lord Jesus Himself, humanly speaking, descended from David—yes, through Abraham via Isaac, but also through Lot via Ruth (who never would have lived apart from Abraham's prayer). And of course, Jesus Christ brought salvation to the world!

Do you see? From Abraham's vantage point, all that appeared in answer to his prayer was a face full of smoke. But in fact, that prayer played a part in the world's salvation.

God can change the world through your prayers as well, even when it seems to you that He's saying no. You just don't know. You have to trust your Father. Let me offer you a practical suggestion:

> Make a list of your requests that God has said no to, especially the most disappointing ones. Take time to talk to God about those requests and re-commit to praying without reserve.

It may be that a huge disappointment comes to mind immediately. Or in your case, it may be a multitude of little things. If you can't think of anything at all, it might be an indicator that you're not praying as specifically as you should.

Your conversation with God will be unique to you—perhaps a plea for help to trust Him and move on past a tragedy. You may want to talk to Him about requests to which the answer is still pending—and has been for many years. The goal of this exercise is to worship God for His fatherly wisdom and move forward toward a place of confidence. If you've settled for just going through the motions of prayer or praying small prayers with little expectation, this is your opportunity to get back on track and begin praying big prayers again (or for the first time) like David, Jabez, and our Lord Jesus.

By the way, kids love to play in dirt piles. I recommend that parents say yes as often as possible. Our heavenly Father likes to say yes as well—and especially huge yeses. If He's had to tell you no, it's most likely that He's planning something even better than you can imagine.

Dear Father, Your ways go beyond my understanding. Many times You haven't answered me the way I expected, and I confess that doubts have come. Even in this season, my faith isn't as strong as I wish it were. But You've never failed me. Every no You've given (and every yes) has been for the best. I praise You for hearing me again and again. I surrender to let You grow me in prayer until I can ask in faith with no reservations. Please train me. I can't wait to see in eternity how much You've done with my prayers. I love You. I pray in Jesus's name, amen.

CONCLUSION

Let me invite you to share one of my burdens.

I'm always moved by Christ's words in Luke 18:8. It's a passage where He's teaching about persevering prayer. He seems to be wrapping up His lesson when He suddenly inserts these sobering words right at the end: "Nevertheless, when the Son of Man comes, will he find faith on earth?"

Do you ever halt in the middle of your Bible reading? Whenever I read this verse, I always feel compelled to stop right there and cry to God, "Yes! Oh, please find faith. Please, Father, give our Lord Jesus the joy and glory of finding a generation with mighty faith to greet Him. Let Him receive the prize of which He is worthy!"

Only one generation will be on earth to welcome Him when He comes. Once He does, that point in history will be fixed forever. When the day has come and gone, what Christ finds will be recorded in permanent ink—for good or bad.

I can't help but think that we might be that generation. Maybe all the hosts of heaven are watching us intently even now, cheering for us to finish well in the final hours. We represent Christ Himself—we are His people. Will Christ get the climactic finale of faith He deserves from us? Will the bride awaiting Him be glorious (Eph. 5:27)?

Even if we're not *that* generation, we're still *a* generation, and our part in Christ's unfolding plans is important. Will the eternal pages of history record that Christ
could do only a few mighty works in our time because
of our unbelief (Matt. 13:58)? Or will He marvel at our
faith (Matt. 8:10)?

I believe, by God's grace, we could experience greater
spiritual awakenings in our day than any previous generation ever has. Whole nations could be changed by the
power of the gospel. The message of Christ could reach
further than ever before into currently unreached people
groups. Young people in our time could live holier, more
powerful, and more devoted lives for Christ than any previous generation of young people.

It all hinges on faith-filled prayer—prayer based on the
Word and character of God.

Does something inside you say, "No. We won't see revival on that scale. Not the way things are going. Not
in my generation"? As you read the stories about Abraham, Jabez, and David, do you think, "I could never attain
that level"? Do you feel like such huge answers to prayer
are a thing of long ago?

If so, you're not alone. Gideon didn't expect to see the
mighty works of old that his fathers had talked about (Judg.
6:13). David himself contrasted the glorious rescues God
had given to his ancestors with his own miserable condition
(Ps. 22:4-6). People in the days of Zechariah the prophet
despised their time as a "day of small things" (Zech 4:10).
But each of those men went on to see the Lord do *big things*.

So can we. The Lord says to us, "Open your mouth wide, and I will fill it" (Ps. 81:10). God's promises haven't changed. His hand hasn't grown short. He invites us to change the world through prayer. The question is not whether God wants to. It's a question of whether we'll respond. Will *you* pray the big prayers? The specific prayers? The bold prayers? The hard prayers? And will you keep on praying?

I've written this book to be a help to you. The stories God has given us are such a help to my own faith, and I hope meditating on them will strengthen you as well. Have you acted on any of the application points? I know it's easy for me to skip the hard "thinking parts" in books, so I chose to give you only one thing to do per chapter. Have you taken the time to try any of those prayer projects? To make them more accessible, I'm listing them in the second appendix for you to reference them.

Recently, I've found it helpful to review the messages of these stories—or at least some of them—in my mind right before my daily prayer time. Here they are in summary so you can keep them in mind as well. Each one is focused on God Himself so you can enter prayer with Him in the forefront of your mind.

1. **God Himself is near**. He has initiated communication with me and is eager for me to respond to Him.

2. **Christ has made the way for me to pray through His own blood**. He values my prayers.

3. **God is my generous Father who loves to bless me**. He intends to make me succeed at His work by means of asking and receiving.

4. **God wants to use me to bless others**. His work is teamwork, and He will give grace to others when I ask.

5. **God hears my prayers**. He will answer them in His perfect timing.

6. **God cares about my feelings**. He sincerely wants me to express my heart to Him.

7. **God has a huge vision**. He will direct me to pray big and specific requests at times, if I depend on His Spirit.

8. **Christ will lead me in praying**. He has set an example, and He will empower me from within to follow Him.

9. **God is a wise Father who knows the best way to respond**. Even when He appears to say no, He will do something wonderful in response to my prayers.

Each numbered point corresponds to the matching chapter number in this book. Do the stories come back to mind as you read through these points? They do for me, and I find this review to be a faith-booster. If these help you as well, perhaps you could print them to hang up around the house or keep with your prayer journal for when it's time to pray. If you need to, you could write in the names of the people that go with each point. May the Lord use what we've studied to make your faith grow and your prayers become stronger for His glory.

God has given us as His people many other books about prayer besides this one. He's given us seminars. And sermons. And biographies of godly prayer warriors. And prayer advances. And prayer rallies. And even prayer apps on our phones!

Perhaps all these blessings are an indictment on us. In spite of so much information, we still don't pray like we should. Ultimately no amount of information is going to produce genuine transformation—which is why we have to actually *seek God* and not just talk about prayer.

But the abundance of resources could be far more than just an indictment. It could be that the Spirit is preparing us for something huge on the horizon. God is moving heart after heart and team after team and church after church to pray. That's why more books keep coming out. More messages are preached. More believers are choosing to gather and cry out for revival.

What part will you play? In *Hear Them Pray* we've heard *them* pray. But now it's your turn. Your generation needs you. Christ has made the way for you. Your heavenly Father waits to listen and answer. He's ready to do *big* things. He's already been doing big things through your prayers, even when you couldn't see it.

So come. Let us draw near to God Himself and pray.

Father, You are faithful. You never disappoint those who trust in You.
I feel that my faith is still so small, but Jesus is worthy of every ounce of it, and I offer it up to You. Please take what faith I have and make it much bigger. I commit to persevere in Your Word and prayer every day and to take my stand as an intercessor. Please use this book to strengthen the faith of everyone who reads it. Please bring a great awakening in our generation that stretches across the world. "Be exalted, O God, above the heavens! Let Your glory be over all the earth!" In Jesus's name, amen.

I love the Lord, because he has heard
my voice and my pleas for mercy.
Because he inclined his ear to me,
therefore I will call on him as long as I live.

Psalm 116:1-2

APPENDIX 1

TEN POINTS ABOUT FASTING

My wife and I did a study of each direct reference in the Bible to fasting, searching for the major themes. Using different colors, we traced the themes we found and then summarized what we learned in the following ten principles about fasting. I'm not including every reference, but these are enough to give you a good sample. For practical ideas, refer back to chapter 6.

The bottom line: God blesses fasting because He gives grace to the humble.

1. **Fasting goes with praying**. (Prayer is the point and the priority. Neh. 1:4–11 and seventeen other passages specifically connect fasting with prayer.)
2. **Fasting is an outward expression of humility**. (1 Kings 21:27–29 and ten other passages specifically demonstrate the connection to humility.)
3. **Fasting adds intensity to prayer and humility**. (Jer. 14:12; Joel 1:13–14; Acts 27:33–38)

4. **Fasting fits best with times of mourning, not times of rejoicing**. (Neh. 9:1; Zech. 7–8; and Matt. 9:14–17 as well as eleven other passages specifically mention mourning in connection to fasting.)

5. **The two primary occasions for fasting are repentance or bringing a specific petition**. (1 Sam. 7:6 is an example of repentance, 2 Chron. 20:3 of petition, and Neh. 1:4 of both.)

6. **Though fasting is not commanded, it seems clear that Christ expected it of His people**. (Matt. 6:16–18; 9:15)

7. **The emphasis of Scripture is that God responds to fasting by answering the request**. (Some examples are 1 Sam. 7:6; Jon. 3:5; and Matt. 6:16–18. See, however, one exception in 2 Sam. 12:16–23.)

8. **After God answers the prayer, you can stop fasting**. (2 Sam. 12:16–23; Zech. 7–8; Acts 27:33–38)

9. **Organized group fasting is good as well as private fasting**. (Judg. 20:26; 2 Chron. 20:3; Acts 13:1–3; 14:23)

10. **God's priority is always on the heart, not on the actual act of fasting**. (The issue is humility, not food: Isa. 58:1–12; Joel 1:14; 2:12–13; Zech. 7:5; 8:19; Luke 18:12.)

APPENDIX 2

SUMMARY OF THE PRAYER PROJECTS

Chapter	Prayer Project	Example	Reference
1	For the next twenty-one days, begin your main prayer time with at least sixty seconds of concentrating on who God is as a person. Purpose to give Him your focused attention and pray as a response to what He has first said to you through His Word.	Abraham	Gen. 18
2	If you have never trusted the Lord Jesus to save you from your sins, refer back to chapter 2. If you have, spend some time praising Him for being the way you can come to God.	The Lord Jesus	John 14:6
3	Prayerfully consider making this resolution: "I resolve not to settle for less in my service to the Lord where He is promising me more. Instead of whispering 'never mind' in the face of impossibilities, I will open my mouth wider" (Ps. 81:10).	Jabez	1 Chron. 4:9-10

Chapter	Prayer Project	Example	Reference
4	Choose some specific blocks of time for intercession and write them into your regular schedule.	Moses	Exod. 17:8-16
5	After each daily prayer time, pause and think of God as your Father responding to you, "Your prayer has been heard."	Zechariah & Elizabeth	Luke 1:5-25
6	Plan a time to fast and pray about a specific matter that Christ lays on your heart.	Hannah	1 Sam. 1-3
7	Begin each daily prayer time by asking the Lord, "What do You want me to pray for?" Then be attentive to the Scriptures and ideas that He brings to mind.	David	Ps. 72:1-20
8	List the following three areas of your prayer life from strongest to weakest: (1) praying for personal victory, (2) praying for powerful ministry, and (3) praying for people you love. For the next month, ask God every day to grow you to be more like Christ in that area where you are weakest (Luke 11:1).	The Lord Jesus	John 11:1-45
9	Make a list of your requests that God has said no to, especially the most disappointing ones. Take time to talk to God about those requests and recommit to praying without reserve.	Abraham	Gen. 19:23-29

NOTES

Introduction
1. By the way, the Lord Jesus was a master at the art of storytelling. In just the Gospel of Luke we find recorded no less than seventeen stories that Jesus told to explain His Father's kingdom. Luke also records Christ's use of nine object lessons, twenty-one analogies, nineteen similes, and forty-five metaphors besides other instances of very imaginative language.

Chapter 2: The Cost of Making a Way
1. See Isaiah 51:17 and Jeremiah 25:15–16.
2. To see the details in the Bible, see John 14:6; Luke 22:39–46; Mark 14:32–42; and Hebrews 12:2.

Chapter 3: Bless Me Too!
1. I considered not using Jabez's story because of the many strong opinions surrounding Bruce Wilkinson's book *The Prayer of Jabez*. But these verses have meant so much to me personally from my own Bible study that I couldn't leave the story out. It captures in a nutshell better than almost any other account the simple call to *ask* God. I waited to read *The Prayer of Jabez* until after I had finished writing this chapter so I could come at it from a fresh perspective and share what God has taught me in my own walk with Him.
2. You can read a fuller account in *Mountain Rain*, a tremendous biography of James Fraser's life by Eileen Crossman. I've been greatly encouraged and influenced by that book.

Chapter 6: God Cares About Our Emotions
1. See Exodus 32:7–14 (Moses) and Hebrews 7:25 (Christ). See also Isaiah 53:12; 59:16; Ezekiel 22:30; and Amos 7:1–6.

Chapter 7: Praying BIG
1. Technically, the Hebrew title could also be translated "Of Solomon," and it is possible that Solomon was the author of Psalm 72. However, many Bible scholars believe David was the author, and I feel the internal evidence compels me to take that position also. One reason is that the first verse speaks of the "royal son," likely a prayer *for* Solomon. Also, the prophetic requests in this chapter correspond to specific fulfillments in Solomon's life. The final line in the psalm is "The prayers of David, the son of Jesse, are ended."
2. Depending on which translation you use, most of the lines from verse 2 and following could sound like statements of fact rather than petitions. The reason is that the Hebrew verb form allows for both ways of translating. However, the context makes it clear, whichever way you translate it, that these are specific requests related to God's blessing on the king and on the kingdom.

Chapter 8: The Master Example
1. See also Luke 3:21; 5:16; 6:12; 9:18, 28; 11:1; 22:39–46.

SPARKS AT TWILIGHT

Flashing in the night
A piece of nothing on fire
Can set worlds ablaze.

J. B. Shepherd is a "piece of nothing," trusting God to be the fire. He wears many hats but aspires above all to be a man of God (2 Tim. 3:17). He and his wife, Marjorie, along with their full quiver of children, live in the Middle East as often as they can.

J. B. is also the author of an allegorical novel, *Anger of the King* (with further books in process to become a series), and a variety of different poems—humorous, romantic, and especially worshipful. You can find his testimony and writings at **SparksAtTwilight.com**.

He would love to hear from you. For personal correspondence, email him at jb@sparksattwilight.com.

ALSO BY J.B. SHEPHERD

Anger of the King

When Adam sides with his grandfather against the king, he hopes to find the approval for which he yearns. Instead, he faces betrayal and the whip of slavery. Desperate, he undertakes a dangerous mission, hoping to regain the king's favor not only for himself but also for Mount Eirene, his home. Meanwhile, Keeda warriors ravage his people's fields, a dragon plots to overthrow the city, and the life or death of all rests in the hands of one man. Can Mount Eirene survive the anger of the king?

Anger of the King is an allegorical novel for young people (and the young at heart), portraying in a captivating way the message of reconciliation with God. Many readers have delighted to see Bible truths come alive and often comment that they recognize their own tendencies in the adventures of young Adam.

Available at Amazon, Kindle, and other platforms.
Find out more at AngeroftheKing.com.

ISBN-13: 978-1-9459763-4-6 | AngeroftheKing.com

FURTHER ENCOURAGEMENT IN PRAYER

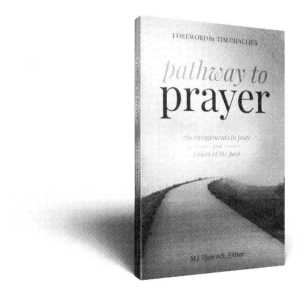

Pathway to Prayer by M. J. Hancock is a tremendous resource if you're looking for further help in your prayer life. Hancock takes some of the best wisdom from some of the godliest writers throughout history and arranges their quotations carefully into a "pathway," just like the title says. The topics move from acknowledging the difficulty with prayer to taking concrete steps that lead into a closer prayer walk with God the Father, the Son, and the Holy Spirit.

ISBN-13: 978-1-9492534-2-9